NomosStudium

Vanessa Sims

English Law and Terminology

Lingua Juris

3. Auflage

Nomos

Die Deutsche Nationalbibliothek verzeichnet diese Publikation in der Deutschen Nationalbibliografie; detaillierte bibliografische Daten sind im Internet über http://dnb.d-nb.de abrufbar.

ISBN 978-3-8329-4951-8

3. Auflage 2010

For Wolfgang

Preface

The law has not escaped the growing globalisation of society: students are increasingly expected to complete their education by studying abroad, and practitioners find themselves confronted with cases containing various foreign elements. Learning foreign law is difficult enough; understanding a completely different legal system is an even bigger challenge. The rules of English law cannot be understood without a firm grasp of the principles of the so-called common law. It is the aim of the first part of this book to provide an accessible introduction to this alien world of case law and precedent, juries and lawyers in wigs. The areas of law outlined in the second part of the book were selected both to illustrate some particular features of the common law, and to cover those subjects foreign lawyers are most likely to encounter.

A book of this size can never do more than offer an introduction to a topic as large as English law; it is hoped that it will provide the reader with the basic understanding and linguistic tools necessary for more detailed study elsewhere. This third edition includes some important developments that have taken place since the second edition was published in 2006. One of the most significant changes introduced by the Constitutional Reform Act 2005 took effect this summer, when the jurisdiction of the House of Lords was transferred to the new Supreme Court. The European Union has expanded again, and faces the challenges brought about by the uncertainty surrounding the Lisbon Treaty. Individual areas of law have also been revised, in some cases leading to greater clarity, in others to new complexities. Many of these changes are ongoing, and this book can once again only present a snap-shot of the law.

As in the previous edition, I am most grateful to my (now former) colleagues at the Norwich Law School who offered their expertise on a variety of chapters. Without them, the task of staying on top of all these momentous developments would have been even harder. As always, thanks are also due to the staff at Nomos Publishers, for their customary speed and professionalism.

Brussels, September 2009

Table of contents

Preface 7

Chapter 1: Characteristics of Legal Language 17

Chapter 2: The Common Law 19
I. Introduction 19
II. The Historical Development of the Common Law 19
1. The Time Before The Norman Conquest 19
2. The Time Following the Norman Conquest 20
3. The Common Law Courts 20
III. Is Common Law Judge-Made Law? 22
IV. The Spread of the Common Law 23
V. Terminology 23
VI. Review and Discussion 24

Chapter 3: Sources of Law 27
I. Minor Sources of Law 27
1. Custom 27
2. Law Merchant 28
3. Canon Law 28
4. Books of Authority 28
II. Major Sources of Law 28
1. Legislation 28
a) Statute Law 28
b) Delegated Legislation 29
c) Statutory Interpretation 30
2. Case Law 30
a) The Rule of Stare Decisis 30
b) Ratio Decidendi and Obiter Dicta 31
c) Distinguishing and Overruling 32
III. Law of the European Community 32
IV. Terminology 32
V. Review and Discussion 34

Chapter 4: The Court System 37
I. Introduction 37
II. The Courts 37
1. Magistrates' Courts 37
2. County Courts 38
3. Crown Court 38
4. High Court of Justice 39
a) The Queen's Bench Division 39
b) The Chancery Division 39
c) The Family Division 39
5. Court of Appeal 40
a) The Civil Division 40
b) The Criminal Division 40

6. The Supreme Court and the House of Lords 40
7. Privy Council 41
III. Simplified Diagram of the Current Court Structure 42
IV. Terminology 42
V. Review and Discussion 43

Chapter 5: Trial System 46
I. The Adversarial System 46
II. The Jury 46
1. Origins of the Jury System 46
2. Composition of the Jury 47
3. Challenging of Jurors and Jury Vetting 47
4. Use of the Jury 48
5. The Role of the Jury 49
III. Terminology 50
IV. Review and Discussion 50

Chapter 6: Legal Personnel 52
I. Judges 52
1. Appointment 52
2. Tenure 52
3. Judicial Independence 53
II. Legal Professions 53
1. Solicitors 53
a) Education and Training 53
b) Work 54
c) The Solicitors Regulation Authority and the Law Society 54
2. Barristers 54
a) Education and Training 54
b) Work 55
c) The Bar Standards Board and the Bar Council 55
III. Law Officers 55
IV. Crown Prosecution Service 56
V. Terminology 56
VI. Review and Discussion 57

Chapter 7: Pre-trial Civil Procedure 60
I. Introduction 60
II. Case Management 60
III. Management Tracks 60
1. Introduction 60
2. Small Claims Track 60
3. Fast Track 61
4. Multi-Track 61
IV. Initiating Proceedings 61
1. Initiating a Claim 61
2. Responding to a Claim 62
3. Statement of Truth 62
V. Disclosure 63

VI. Evidence 63
VII. Judgment Without Trial 63
1. Default Judgment 63
2. Summary Judgment 63
VIII. Legal Aid 64
IX. Terminology 64
X. Review and Discussion 65

Chapter 8: Constitutional Law 67
I. Nature of the Constitution 67
1. The Unwritten Constitution 67
2. Constitutional Conventions 67
II. Important Constitutional Principles 67
1. The Rule of Law 67
2. The Royal Prerogative 68
3. Parliamentary Sovereignty 69
4. The Doctrine of Separation of Powers 70
III. Parliament 70
1. Introduction 70
2. The House of Commons 70
3. The House of Lords 71
4. Government 72
5. The Legislative Process 72
IV. Devolution 73
V. Terminology 74
VI. Review and Discussion 76

Chapter 9: Equity and Trusts 78
I. Historical Development of Equity 78
1. Development of the Court of Chancery 78
2. The Fusion of Law and Equity 79
II. Maxims of Equity 79
1. Nature of Equitable Maxims 79
2. Examples of Equitable Maxims 79
III. Equitable Remedies 80
1. Introduction 80
2. Specific Performance 80
3. Injunctions 80
a) Prohibitory and Mandatory Injunctions 80
b) Final and Interim Injunctions 81
c) Without Notice Injunctions 81
d) Freezing Injunctions and Search Orders 81
4. Rescission 81
5. Rectification 81
IV. Trusts 82
1. Historical Development of the Trust 82
2. Definition of the Trust 83
3. The Private Express Trust 83
4. Purpose Trusts 84

5. Charitable Trusts 84
6. Constructive and Resulting Trusts 84
7. Fiduciary Duties 85
8. Tracing 85
V. Terminology 85
VI. Review and Discussion 86

Chapter 10: Contract Law 88
I. Introduction 88
II. Formation of a Contract 88
1. Freedom of Contract 88
2. Offer and Acceptance 88
3. Consideration 89
4. Form 90
5. Intention to Create Legal Relations 90
III. Contents of the Contract 90
1. Express and Implied Terms 90
2. Conditions, Warranties and Innominate Terms 91
3. Standard Form Contracts 91
IV. Contracts and Third Parties 92
1. Privity of Contract and the Contract (Rights of Third Parties) Act 1999 92
2. Agency 92
V. Void and Voidable Contracts 92
1. Meaning of 'Void' and 'Voidable' 92
2. Capacity 93
3. Illegality 93
4. Mistake 93
5. Misrepresentation 94
6. Duress and Undue Influence 94
a) Duress 94
b) Undue Influence 94
VI. End of the Contract 95
1. Performance 95
2. Breach 95
3. Frustration 95
VII. Remedies 95
1. Damages 95
2. Specific Performance 96
3. Restitution 96
VIII. Terminology 96
IX. Review and Discussion 97

Chapter 11: The Law of Tort 99
I. Introduction 99
II. Fundamental Principles of Tortious Liability 99
1. Introduction 99
2. Causation 99
3. Remoteness 100
4. Contributory Negligence 100

III. Main Torts 100
1. Defamation 100
2. Nuisance 101
a) Private Nuisance 101
b) Public Nuisance 101
3. Trespass 102
4. Strict Liability: The Rule in Rylands v Fletcher 102
5. Negligence 103
IV. Remedies 104
1. Introduction 104
2. Damages 104
V. Defences 105
1. Introduction 105
2. General Defences 105
3. Special Defences 105
VI. Terminology 106
VII. Review and Discussion 107

Chapter 12: Commercial Law 109
I. Commercial Law 109
II. Introduction to Sale of Goods Law 109
1. Definition of Contract of Sale 109
2. Subject-Matter of the Contract 110
a) Definition of 'Goods' 110
b) Classification of Goods 111
III. Duties of the Seller 111
1. Duty to Pass Good Title 111
2. Duty to Deliver 111
3. Duty to Deliver Goods at the Right Time 112
4. Duty to Supply the Right Quantity of Goods 112
5. Duty to Supply Goods of the Right Quality 113
IV. Duties of the Buyer 113
1. Duty to Pay the Price 113
2. Duty to Accept the Goods 114
V. Effects of the Contract 114
1. Transfer of Property 114
2. Passing of Risk 114
VI. Remedies 115
1. Remedies of the Seller 115
2. Remedies of the Buyer 116
VII. Terminology 116
VIII. Review and Discussion 117

Chapter 13: Company Law 119
I. Introduction 119
II. Birth of a Company 119
1. Nature of Registered Companies 119
2. Classification of Companies 119
3. Formalities and Documentation 120

III. People Involved 120
1. Promoters 120
2. Directors 120
3. Secretary 121
IV. Membership 121
V. Shares 121
1. Introduction 121
2. Types of Shares 122
VI. Capital 122
VII. General Meetings 123
VIII. Shareholder Remedies 123
IX. Winding-up 124
X. Terminology 124
XI. Review and Discussion 125

Chapter 14: European Union Law 127
I. The European Communities 127
II. The Political Institutions of the EC 128
1. The Commission 128
2. The Council 128
3. The European Parliament 129
4. The Economic and Social Committee and the Committee of the Regions 129
5. The Court of Auditors 129
III. The Legislative Process 129
1. The Consultation Procedure 129
2. The Co-operation Procedure 130
3. The Co-decision Procedure 130
IV. The Judicial Institutions of the EC 130
1. The European Court of Justice 130
2. The Court of First Instance 131
V. EC Law 131
1. Sources of EC Law 131
2. Community Legislation 132
3. General Principles of Law 132
VI. The EC and the Member States 133
1. Introduction 133
2. Direct Effect 133
3. Article 234 References (formerly Article 177 References) 134
VII. Substantive EC law 134
1. Free Movement of Goods 134
2. Free Movement of Workers 135
3. Freedom of Establishment and Free Movement of Services 135
4. Free Movement of Capital 135
VIII. Terminology 136
IX. Review and Discussion 137

Chapter 15: Other Areas of Law 139
I. Classifications of Law 139
II. Other Areas of Law 139
III. Terminology 141

Index 143

Chapter 1: Characteristics of Legal Language

Language and communication lie at the very heart of the law. The parliamentary draftsman, the lawyer, the client, the judge, all have to make their meaning understood, whether orally or in writing. Like most professions, the law has developed its own language; learning to use it correctly is an integral part of learning the law itself. The advantage of such 'professional jargon' is that it enables lawyers to communicate in an effective and efficient way; the disadvantage is that lay people are often unable to understand it.

One of the main characteristics of legal language is the use of **terms of art**. These are words which have a precise legal definition; they thus convey a clear meaning to a lawyer, but not to a lay person. Someone who is not legally qualified may well recognise the word **tort** as being a legal one, but he may not know that it can be defined as a civil wrong independent of contract. Some terms of art, such as **claimant**, **defendant** and **appeal**, apply to the whole body of the law, while others are used in a particular area only. Examples of the latter are **consideration** in contract law, **murder** in criminal law and **trustee** in the law of trusts.

Many terms which are regularly used by lawyers are not sufficiently precise to be classed as terms of art, but are nevertheless recognisable as being specific to the legal community. Such words are referred to as **argot**, *i.e.* a language or jargon that members of a particular group use to communicate with each other. The advantage of such terms is that they can be used to avoid lengthy explanations. Thus every lawyer knows that **'Blackacre'** and **'Whiteacre'** refer to fictitious pieces of land, which are used in order to avoid reference to actual property.

Most examples of terms of art and argot are words which are not used in common parlance. However, a further characteristic of the language of the law is that ordinary words can have a different meaning in a legal context. A **party** is therefore not a celebration, but a person who has entered into a contract or is involved in a law suit. Law suit, incidentally, is the legal meaning of the word **action**. An **instrument** is a legal document, which is said to be **executed** when it is signed and delivered to the recipient, and **consideration** refers not to a degree of thought, but to something which must be given by one person to make the promise of another legally binding.

When the French language was introduced into England following the Norman Conquest of 1066, the main language of the law was not English, but Latin. With the development of royal (and therefore French-speaking) courts a situation arose in which all three languages were used in court proceedings. Many people did not speak either Latin or French, and would therefore state their case and present their evidence in English. Lawyers' arguments and the decision of the court would be in French, and the law report would be in Latin. Finally the judgment had to be translated back into English, so that the parties could understand what had been decided. Legal expressions in all three languages were therefore used simultaneously, and it is not surprising that both Latin and French have had a lasting influence on legal English.

The frequent use of Latin terms and phrases, such as **ratio decidendi** and **obiter dicta,** is a distinctive feature of legal language in England and Wales, but its usage has been discouraged in recent years as fewer and fewer pupils receive Latin lessons at school. However, common Latin phrases such as **curia advisari vult**, used in law reports to indicate that the court took time to consider the judgment, and **bona fide,** meaning good faith, will continue to feature in legal documents and reports.

The French influence can be seen in the origin of words like **laches**, and there are even some French expressions still in use today. Examples include **in lieu** ('instead of') and the estate **pur autre vie** (a type of proprietary interest in land, the duration of which is determined by the life of another person).

Chapter 2: The Common Law

I. Introduction

The term **common law** carries several meanings but it is important to note than in this context the word 'common' does not bear its usual meaning of 'vulgar' or 'ordinary'. Historically, it refers to "the law common to all the land", a body of rules that developed in contrast to local customs. Over time, the term also came to be used to distinguish this law of the land from specialised areas of law, such as ecclesiastical law, the law merchant and equity. Furthermore, 'common law' is a synomym for case law, that is law created by decisions of the courts as opposed to law created by statute. Finally, the term also describes a legal system which differs significantly from the **civil law systems** of most continental countries. The basic difference between these two legal traditions is that civil law systems are centred around codes, while common law systems focus on case law and individual statutes.

II. The Historical Development of the Common Law

There is no fixed date in history that marks the inception of English law. Centuries of social development mean that little now remains of the origins of the law, but many characteristics of the modern English legal system are still best understood in the light of their historical evolution.

The history of the common law is very much the history of its institutions, as the common law was the law applied by the common law courts, and it charts the development and increasing complexity of society. One of the first areas to emerge was criminal law, with offences like **breach of the peace** providing an efficient means of preserving public, and thus social, order. The laws relating to contracts, torts and land are also very old and served to reinforce key elements of feudal society. Other principles evolved to reflect more recent economic and cultural changes; for example, the main growth of commercial law took place in the late eighteenth century, a time when commerce and trade expanded tremendously.

1. The Time Before The Norman Conquest

The earliest written records on customs in early England are of **Roman** origin. The Romans brought with them their own advanced system of law. However, this did not prevail in England after their withdrawal at the beginning of the fifth century. Instead **Celtic** customs continued to dominate as they had since the Celtic invasions in the Bronze and Iron Ages. Over the next few centuries important influences were added by new conquerors, such as the **Angles**, **Saxons** and **Danes**.

At this stage England was far from being a unified country. It was divided into several kingdoms, some large and some small. The process of unification, commenced by Alfred of Wessex in the ninth century, was completed in the tenth century. However, this did not immediately lead to the development of an equally uniform system of law. The country was divided into **shires**, many of which remain virtually unchanged as the **counties** of modern England. The shires were sub-divided into **hundreds**, which again consisted of several smaller units. Disputes were resolved at regular **assemblies** in the shires and hundreds, e.g. the **shire-moot**. However, these meetings did not resemble present-day courts. They combined administrative, legislative and judicial functions and there were no fixed rules as to procedure or evidence.

Trial by ordeal was a widespread practice. This involved an appeal to God, that He might resolve the disputes of men. In England it normally took the form of **fire** or **water**. If the party involved passed the ordeal God was taken to have decided in his favour. Apart from trial by ordeal local customs remained varied. They also remained largely unwritten, despite the efforts of several individual kings, who tried to compile written laws.

2. The Time Following the Norman Conquest

In 1066 England was conquered by the **Normans** under William, Duke of Normandy, who came to be known as William the Conqueror. This event is often regarded as decisive for the development of the common law. While it is true that the Normans introduced important changes it has to be remembered that they did not bring a unified system of law with them, nor did they intentionally develop the common law. On the contrary, the first changes actually further diversified the law. Ecclesiastical courts were separated from the courts of the shires and hundreds; **trial by battle** and discrimination between the French and the English were introduced.

The main aim of the new king and his successors was to tighten their hold over the country. Members of the main advisory body of the monarch, the ***Curia Regis***, began to travel the country and dispense **royal justice** – the law of the king. The following provides a good example of how the development of the king's law served to strengthen the authority of the Crown. The lesser lords of England were constantly fighting amongst themselves, the winner increasing his power by taking over the land of the loser. In 1166 the **Assize of Novel Disseisin** provided that a person who had been dispossessed of his land could obtain a remedy in the new **royal courts**, *i.e.* the winner had to return the land to the original owner. It was therefore no longer profitable for the lords to fight each other; thus there was less risk of one lord becoming powerful enough to challenge the king. The second incentive for the Crown was of a financial nature. Criminal law was especially profitable, as fines and forfeitures went to the king.

Royal justice was accepted by the people because it provided more effective procedures and methods of enforcement than the traditional courts in the shires and hundreds. In addition, a central written record for royal cases was devised in the late twelfth century. This meant that once a dispute was resolved and written down there could be no doubt as to what the decision had been and no risk of the case being reopened by one of the parties.

The fact that royal justice was advantageous for both the Crown and private litigants lead to the rapid growth of this new type of law, which became known as the 'common law'. King Henry II, who reigned from 1154 to 1189, was especially active in developing the common law and reducing the importance of the shire and hundred courts. In time the workload of the king's judges became too great for the *Curia Regis*. Its legal functions were therefore separated from its administrative and advisory role and taken over by the new common law courts.

3. The Common Law Courts

The first of the **common law courts** was the **Court of Exchequer**. The **Exchequer** was the **treasury**, one of the two important departments of state which had come into existence within the first century after the Norman conquest (the other being the Chancery, which will be discussed in detail below). The name is derived from the table used to count taxes, which was chequered – black and white like a chessboard. The Court of Exchequer was responsible for all **financial** and **revenue matters.** The **Court of Assize** dealt with both criminal and civil matters. It was divided into areas, the so-called **circuits** and **itinerant judges** would travel from one circuit to another. Disputes between individuals that did not concern royal rights were the responsibility of the **Court of Common Pleas.** A large part of its workload consisted of cases involving land. It did not hear criminal cases. The jurisdiction of the **Court of King's Bench** was based on offences committed against the king's peace and developed to cover both criminal and civil cases. In addition it had a supervisory function, as it could hear appeals from lower courts and control royal officials by way of **prerogative writs** (which are still issued today). The writ of ***certiorari*** transferred a case from a lower court to the Court of King's Bench, **prohibition** prevented a lower court from exceeding its jurisdiction and ***mandamus*** compelled a court or public officer to carry out his duty.

An important point in the development of the common law, which took place before the final division of the *Curia Regis*, was the signing of the **Magna Carta** in 1215. John, who succeeded Richard I and was king from 1199 to 1216, was one of the most unpopular monarchs of all time. The barons of England eventually threatened to withdraw their **fealty** from John and take up arms against him if he did not grant a charter of rights. The Magna Carta laid down several constitutional and legal principles of profound importance. For example, it stated that the Court of Common Pleas should in future be held in a fixed place. Until then the Court had followed the king on his journeys through the country, which lead to severe inconvenience and expenditure for those who wished to bring cases there. Following the granting of the charter the Court of Common Pleas was established in Westminster and remained there until its abolition. Furthermore justice was not to be sold, denied or delayed to anyone, and when appointing justices the king was to ensure that they knew the law and intended to observe it. All in all the Magna Carta imposed notable restrictions on the prerogative powers of the king and significantly influenced the development of the law.

During all this time the importance of the old courts was gradually diminishing, until they virtually disappeared. The next few centuries saw important changes both in law and politics, with the development of Parliament and a sharp rise in the number of statutes passed. However, there was relatively little change in the way the law was administered, as the existing court structure remained the same. It was not until the end of the fifteenth century and the reign of Henry VII (1485 to 1509) that a new court was introduced. This was the **Court of Star Chamber,** which dealt mostly with criminal cases, such as riots and conspiracies. Opinions differ as to whether defendants and/or witnesses were tortured during the trial, but it is undisputed that the punishments imposed by the Chamber were often very severe. The most common punishment were heavy fines (often amounting to several thousand pounds), but defendants were also regularly **pilloried,** imprisoned and mutilated (for example by having their ears cut off, noses slit or cheeks branded). These harsh sentences lead to the growing unpopularity of the Court of Star Chamber and it was eventually abolished in 1641.

The reign of Henry VIII (1509 to 1547) was dominated to some extent by England's split from the Roman Catholic Church, which lead to fundamental changes in the relationship between state and church. Legal changes included the establishment of several new specialist courts and the development of land law, but still the main court structure remained unaltered. The next few centuries saw major political, social and legal changes during the **Civil Wars, Interregnum, Restoration** and the **Glorious Revolution**. The Interregnum was lead by **Oliver Cromwell**, who introduced some significant reforms (such as making English, rather than French, the official language of the law) and contemplated many more (including acquittal for justifiable homicide and the creation of local courts). Unfortunately none of these changes survived the Restoration.

It was not until the middle of the nineteenth century, under Queen Victoria, that the idea of local courts was taken up again. Most litigants still had to bear the inconvenience of travelling to London, until a new type of local court, the **county courts**, were introduced in 1846. At first their jurisdiction was limited to claims involving less than £20, but this limit was soon increased considerably. The reign of Queen Victoria, which lasted from 1837 to 1901, saw other important developments, for example in land law, the law of torts and criminal law. The main change in the court system, however, was brought about by the **Judicature Acts 1873–75**, which established the hierarchy of courts in its present form. The old common law courts of Exchequer, King's Bench and Common Pleas were finally abolished and their jurisdiction transferred to the new **High Court**. Only the new county courts and the Court of Assize remained unchanged, the latter finally being abolished in 1971. The modern court system will be discussed in detail below.

III. Is Common Law Judge-Made Law?

The question whether or not the common law was 'made' (*i.e.* made up) by the early royal judges is mainly of theoretical and historical interest only, as the common law is now a widespread and firmly established system of law, regardless of its origins. Nevertheless a short look will be taken at this issue.

At the time the first royal judges started travelling the country local customs were extremely diverse. It is more than likely that itinerant judges would refer to and be influenced by these customs when deciding cases brought before them. This led to the claim that the judges only 'discovered' the common, popular law; that they toured the country, found out what the custom was and declared what the law had always been. However, this is a distorted picture of the work of the royal judges. They did not just articulate existing practices, they did actively develop the law. This can be seen by looking at the test that judges used to decide whether a local habit did in fact qualify as a custom in the legal sense. There are a number of requirements that a custom must fulfil in order to be recognised as having legal force. One of these is that the practice must be reasonable. What was reasonable in the circumstances was for the judge to decide. If a judge did not like a particular custom, he could declare it to be unreasonable and therefore not a custom in the legal sense at all. This clearly shows that the first royal judges could decide whether or not to follow a custom and could so influence the development of the law in a certain direction. The early common law was therefore to a certain degree judge-made law.

Today the situation is very different. Most new law is created by statute, and judges would vigorously deny the charge that they are 'making law'. Nevertheless they do retain a significant amount of discretion, and judicial activism will always be a prominent feature of the common law.

IV. The Spread of the Common Law

"The common law is the law common to all the land." This sentence naturally raises the question what exactly 'all the land' is referring to. Does it refer only to England? What about Wales, Scotland and Northern Ireland? In this context it is very important to distinguish between geography and politics on the one hand and the law on the other.

Geographically and politically there is a close link between the individual countries. **England**, **Scotland** and **Wales** together form what is known as **Great Britain**. Great Britain and **Northern Ireland** make up the **United Kingdom of Great Britain and Northern Ireland**. A special position is occupied by the four **Channel Islands** Jersey, Guernsey, Alderney and Sark and the **Isle of Man** as so-called **separate dependencies** of the British Crown. As far as the law is concerned there is no such close link between the countries. The term **English law** always refers to the law of England and Wales, as these two countries share the same legal system and the same individual laws. Scotland, in contrast, has a **hybrid system** that is based partly on the common law and partly on Roman law. It would therefore be more accurate to speak of 'English and Welsh law', but the reference to Wales is normally omitted. Northern Ireland and Scotland are not included in any discussion of 'English law' and must be kept separate. The same applies to the Channel Islands and the Isle of Man. In the following only the law of England and Wales will be discussed, unless otherwise stated.

The **British Empire** was the medium through which the common law system was spread all over the world, from North America over Africa to Asia and Australia. Virtually all former colonies are now completely independent, and some have been for a considerable time, such as the United States of America, which declared its independence in 1776. Nevertheless many remained strongly influenced by English law. The list includes the United States, Canada, Australia, New Zealand, Nigeria, Kenya and many others. In fact about a third of the world's population lives in countries whose legal system has been influenced by the common law to a greater or lesser degree.

It should be remembered that this refers to the way the legal system of these countries is organised, such as the sources of law, the court structure and the legal professions. It does not necessarily mean that the laws are exactly the same as in England. The laws were very similar at the beginning and for a long time the courts in these countries were bound by decisions of English courts. Many courts, such as the Australian ones, continued to follow the decisions of English courts, even after they were no longer obliged to do so. Over time, however, the former colonies began to deviate from English cases and to develop their own law and courts of appeal. The number of countries who accept an English court as their highest court of appeal has declined steadily over recent years, with New Zealand the most recent country to sever this link.

V. Terminology

Breach of the peace: an act such as assault or riot, which threatens the peace and security of an individual or the public.

Civil law system: refers to a legal system which is based on Roman law and centres around codes. Examples include French and German law. In a different context 'civil law' can also refer to private law, as opposed to, for example, criminal law.

Civil Wars: the **Civil Wars** (1642 – 1648) arose out of the continuing conflict between Crown and Parliament. Charles I was a very unpopular monarch, who was accused by many of arbitrary government and imposing illegal taxation. Matters escalated when he tried to arrest some of his opponents in Parliament. Civil war broke out and the **Royalists** were finally defeated by the Parliamentary forces, and Charles I was tried before a court and executed. In 1653 Oliver Cromwell became the **Lord Protector** of the country.

Counties: England is divided into a number of **counties**, which are part of the local government structure. Each **county** is subdivided into **districts**. The close link between old shires and modern counties can be seen in names such as Yorkshire, Cambridgeshire and Leicestershire.

Fealty: the tenant was bound to his feudal lord by fealty, an oath of fidelity. This imposed various duties on the tenant, for example not to harm the lord.

Glorious Revolution: James II (1685 – 1689) tried to restore Roman Catholicism, a move hugely unpopular with influential parliamentarians and the Church. They responded by offering the Crown to (the Protestant) William of Orange and his wife Mary. James II fled to France and was said to have abdicated. He was the last absolute ruler, as William accepted the Bill of Rights. The course of events which led to the establishment of William and Mary as monarchs is called the Glorious Revolution.

Interregnum: the period of time between the execution of Charles I and the Restoration, during which England was a Republic and Oliver Cromwell Lord Protector of the country.

Pillory: a wooden frame, in which the offender's head and hands were locked. He was then exposed in a public place for ridicule and molestation.

Restoration: following Cromwell's death the monarchy was restored, the Crown being offered to Charles II. This period was called the **Restoration**, and many of the changes introduced by Cromwell were undone.

Trial by battle: retained the idea of divine judgment. The two parties would fight, and the winner was considered to have been granted victory by God.

Trial by Ordeal: based on the notion that God would interfere in the disputes of men to reveal the guilt or innocence of the accused. The most common forms were **ordeal by fire** and **ordeal by water.** The former involved inflicting burns on a person, for example by requiring him to carry a piece of red hot metal a certain distance. If the burns healed within three days, he was considered innocent. An accused subjected to trial by water was bound with a rope and lowered into water. If he sank he was innocent, if he floated he was guilty.

VI. Review and Discussion

1. *What are the different meanings of the term 'the common law'?*

Originally 'common law' referred to the law 'common to all the land', thus distinguishing it from local customs. Over time, however, the term has acquired several other meanings. It can be used to differentiate between different systems of law, such as ecclesiastical law, the law merchant and equity. Ecclesiastical law has long been completely separate, and the law merchant has been assimilated into commercial law, but the distinction between common law and equity remains relevant even today. It is also important to differentiate between statute law and common law, which in this context is synonymous with case law. Although most new law is introduced by way of legislation, many legal principles are still common law rules. Finally, 'common law' can refer to a legal system, which can be contrasted with civil law systems. Civilian systems, such as those of France and Germany, are strongly influenced by Roman law. Individual rules are collected together in codes, and although cases are important, they are not binding on later decisions. Common law systems rely much more on case law (decided cases are binding under the rule of precedent) and individual statutes.

2. *Explain the term 'common law courts'.*

After the Norman Conquest members of the king's advisory body, the *Curia Regis*, started to travel around the country, applying royal justice. This was the first time that law was applied uniformly throughout the land, and it became known as the common law. The new law provided better procedures and more effective methods of enforcement than the old shire and hundred courts, and as an increasing number of people relied on royal justice, use of the traditional system slowly declined. Over time the workload became too great for the *Curia Regis*, which also had extensive advisory and administrative functions. The task of dispensing the king's law was therefore taken over by the new common law courts. These were the Court of Exchequer (financial and revenue matters), the Court of Assize (criminal and civil matters), the Court of Common Pleas (civil cases, mainly relating to land) and the Court of King's Bench (civil and criminal cases and supervisory function). This court system remained virtually unchanged until the Judicature Acts 1873-75 (with the exception of the creation and abolition of the Court of Star Chamber, and the creation of the county courts). Most of the old common law courts were superseded by the new High Court, with the exception of the Court of Assize, which existed until 1971.

3. *How did the legal professions develop?*

It is not easy to outline the history of the legal professions. Changes took place over long periods of time, with no clear beginning or end, and contrasting developments often overlapped. The problem is compounded by the scarcity of available records. The following can therefore only present a much simplified account of this aspect of legal history.

The increasing technicality and complexity of legal proceedings led to a growing demand for men who were experts at dealing with court cases. A basic distinction developed between **attorneys**, who represented a litigant in his absence (acting effectively as agents), and **pleaders**, who took over the oral presentation of the case. In the thirteenth century the profession of pleader began to be recognised and regulated and in the fourteenth century a number of pleaders founded the small but influential guild of **serjeants-at-law**. They had exclusive audience before the Court of Common Pleas, and over time it became established that only serjeants could be appointed as judges.

Another important group of lawyers were the **apprentices-at-law**. Despite their name, they were not merely students, but recognised advocates who ranked below the serjeants. They obtained their knowledge directly from the courts, rather than one of the universities, and acted as private advisors and advocates in courts other than Common Pleas.

Gradually responsibility for the education of lawyers was taken over by the **Inns of Court**. These originated as living quarters and developed into centres of social activity and learning. Four Inns, namely Gray's Inn, Lincoln's Inn, Inner Temple and Middle Temple, became dominant. These four still exist today, but little is known about Inns of lesser status, although some of them existed until Victorian times.

Over time apprentices began to erode the pre-eminent position of serjeants, for example by gaining the right to judicial appointment and, in 1846, the right to appear before the Court of Common Pleas. No more serjeants were created, and the order was dissolved in 1877.

The term **barrister** originated in the Inns of Court in the fifteenth century. Initially, it was used only internally to describe apprentices who had gained prominence in relation to the mock trials, the so-called **moot courts**, which were a prominent feature of legal education in the Inns.

Solicitors also gained prominence in the fifteenth century. They provided a wide range of quasi-legal services, such as advising clients on preliminary issues of jurisdiction and dealing with attorneys and advocates. Their role became increasingly concerned with offering professional legal services and by the seventeenth century solicitors were recognised as a further branch of the profession.

Chapter 3: Sources of Law

I. Minor Sources of Law

Some sources that were very important during the development of the common law, like the law merchant, have lost most of their direct influence by being assimilated into the common law. Others, such as books of authority, are **minor sources** because they are used to supplement the two major (or primary) sources, case law and statute.

It can be disputed whether **Roman law** should be included in the list of minor sources of English law. Its influence was only indirect; Roman law was never applied as such by any courts. It will therefore not be included in the following discussion.

1. Custom

The term **custom** has three different meanings. Firstly, it refers to the basis of the common law itself. As was stated above, the common law was not a new set of laws introduced by the Normans, it was developed on the basis of existing customs and laws. These customs have been incorporated into the common law and are therefore not a separate source of law.

Secondly, custom can mean **trade usages,** *i.e.* the way things are normally done in a certain business community. The courts can sometimes imply terms into contracts on the basis of such trade usages. However, as this is more a question of fact than a question of law, custom in the meaning of trade usage is also not a proper source of law.

Thirdly, the term custom describes traditions or usages which have become **rules of law** in a certain defined **locality** (and only there). In this sense customs are a separate source of law. A common example is a **right of way,** *i.e.* the right of one landowner to walk across the property of another in order to get to, for example, a road.

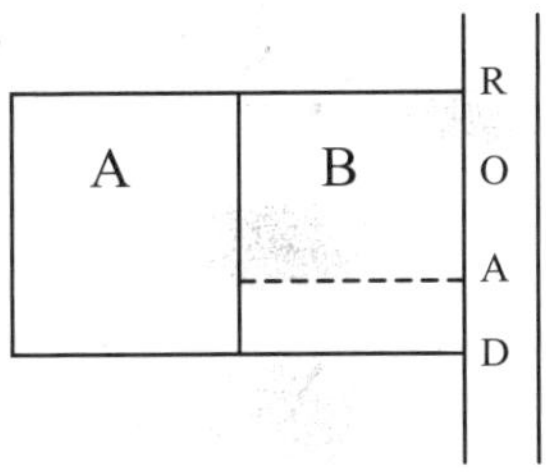

Diagram of a right of way. A can use the path across B's property in order to get to the road.

A local usage will only be accepted by the courts as a legal custom if the person claiming a right under that custom can show that it satisfies a test that includes the following requirements.

(I) **Antiquity:** The custom must have existed since **time immemorial.** The starting point of 'time immemorial' has been fixed by statute at 1189, the first year of the reign of Richard I. As it will normally be impossible to prove that the custom has existed since 1189 it is sufficient to prove that the custom has existed for a long time. The courts will then presume that it has existed since time immemorial. This presumption can be rebutted if it is shown that there was a time when it was impossible to exercise the right in question (for example because there once was a lake where the right of way is being claimed).

(II) Certainty: The custom must be **certain.** The owner of a right of way, for example, will normally only be entitled to cross the adjoining property by a certain route, such as a path.

(III) Reasonableness: One of the most important requirements is that the custom in question must be **reasonable.** A right of way to get to a road, for example, will not be reasonable, if the person claiming it can easily access the same road from his own property.

2. Law Merchant

As overseas trade expanded and England developed into a shipping and merchant country it became evident that the very rudimentary principles of contract law as applied in the common law courts were inadequate for dealing with the increasing amount of litigation in this area. The problem was solved by the development of a new set of courts which dealt exclusively with matters arising from the merchant community, such as disputes concerning trade customs and maritime practices. The law applied by these courts became known as the **law merchant.** Many rules and doctrines of the law merchant were later assimilated into the common law and can now be found in commercial law.

3. Canon Law

The **canon law** is the law of the Catholic Church. Many important concepts of the common law can be traced to canon law, such as the close link between criminal law and morality and the protection that the law gives to the institutions of marriage and family.

Canon law has also had a more direct influence as a source of English law through the ecclesiastical courts, which were completely separate from the common law courts. Constant clashes between Church and State over questions of absolute authority lead to a gradual decline of the jurisdiction of the ecclesiastical courts, until they were finally limited to matters affecting members of the Church.

4. Books of Authority

For centuries **legal treatises** written by famous jurists, such as **Coke** and **Blackstone,** have shaped the law. The citation of **books of authority** used to be restricted by the rule that the author of a book had to be dead before it was considered to be an authority and could be cited in court. This rule has been abolished and newer books are now also regularly cited **in argument.**

II. Major Sources of Law

1. Legislation

a) Statute Law

Most 'new' law is enacted in the form of **statutes** (also known as **primary legislation**). These **Acts of Parliament** are passed by the legislature according to certain rules of procedure and must receive Royal Assent before they become binding law. **Statute law** prevails over common law, so if there is a conflict between the two, the courts must follow the Act of Parliament.

In England Parliament can pass any statute on any subject matter. This is what is known as parliamentary sovereignty, and will be discussed in more detail below. One of the practical consequences of this doctrine is that no court in England has the power to declare Acts of Parliament **void**; there is no **constitutional court** like in many other countries, which measures statutes against some form of higher law embodied in a written constitution. Provided that the correct procedure for passing an Act of Parliament has been observed, all the courts can do is **interpret** and **apply** individual statutes.

A slight change to this rule was created by the **Human Rights Act 1998**. If a court finds that an Act infringes human rights (broadly as set out in the European Convention on Human Rights), it can issue a **declaration of incompatibility**. In most cases Parliament will respond quickly to alter the relevant provisions, but it does not have to do so. The courts' power is limited to a formal declaration; they cannot themselves alter the wording of the statute, nor can they force Parliament or Government to act. The Human Rights Act 1998 therefore does not present a real challenge to the doctrine of parliamentary sovereignty. However, although the courts cannot 'strike down' Acts that infringe human rights, they do have very wide and novel powers of interpretation which they are required to use so that potentially incompatible Acts are read and given effect to in a way that makes them compatible "so far as it is possible to do so".

The inability of the courts to affect the **validity** of Acts of Parliament should not be confused with their ability to review actions of the state. If a public body acts illegally, then the courts can intervene and declare the action in question to be void. This is called **judicial review** and is an important part of administrative law.

b) Delegated Legislation

Parliament can **delegate** some of its legislative power to subordinate bodies, thus enabling them to pass their own **rules, regulations** and **by-laws**. This is often necessary, because Parliament cannot deal with all matters in detail. A statute will therefore set out a **legislative framework**, while details of implementation and application are dealt with by **delegated legislation** (also known as **subordinate** or **secondary legislation**). This not only saves parliamentary time, but also provides flexibility, as such rules and regulations can be more easily adapted to deal with unforeseen problems than an Act of Parliament.

There are various kinds of delegated legislation. **Orders** and regulations, which are often issued by a Minister or Government department, are collectively referred to as **statutory instruments**. The highest form of delegated legislation are **Orders in Council**, which are issued by the Privy Council (consisting of the Sovereign and the Privy Councillors). Local authorities are often granted the power to make by-laws to regulate and administrate certain activities in their area.

One of the main problems with delegated legislation is the loss of parliamentary control over legislation. However, the statute in which power is delegated away from Parliament must specify what the subordinate body can and cannot do. Delegated legislation must remain within the boundaries set by this **enabling statute** (sometimes referred to as the **parent act**). It is then called ***intra vires*** and has the same force as Acts of Parliament. Delegated legislation which exceeds the powers conferred by Parliament is ***ultra vires*** and therefore inoperative.

c) Statutory Interpretation

An Act of Parliament cannot cover in detail all possible situations to which it might apply in the future; it can only provide a broad legal framework. Statutes are therefore often drafted in a fairly general way, so that they can cover a variety of different situations. However, this means that they must be **interpreted** before they can be applied to an individual case. The broad language used also often leads to uncertainty or ambiguity, which increases the need for **judicial interpretation**.

The courts receive some help in this task from the **Interpretation Act 1978**, which lays down a number of general principles, such as the rule that, unless otherwise stated, the male gender includes the female and the singular includes the plural. Some statutes also have their own **interpretation sections**. However, these aids are not sufficient to deal with all problems of interpretation.

The courts have developed so-called **rules of interpretation**, which provide some uniformity in the way in which Acts of Parliament are constructed. These rules are not binding, but rather illustrate the general approaches takes by the courts. They act as guidelines, and it is up to the court to decide which rule is the most appropriate in a given case. There are three main rules of interpretation.

The **literal rule** requires that, if the words used in the statute are plain and unambiguous, they should be given their plain, ordinary and grammatical meaning. However, in some cases the literal interpretation of words might lead to absurdity. According to the **golden rule** the ordinary meaning of words can be modified in these cases; the court can chose an interpretation which avoids the absurdity. The same applies if the literal interpretation of words would lead to inconsistency within the Act. The **mischief rule**, finally, takes a more purposive approach. The court looks at the mischief, *i.e.* the defect in the law which the statute aims to remedy, and adopts the interpretation which is best suited for achieving that objective.

There are also some subsidiary rules of interpretation. An example is the ***eiusdem generis* rule**: where general words follow specific words, the general words must be applied to the meaning of the specific words. If an Act refers to 'dogs, cats and other animals' the general term (other animals) must be interpreted in line with the specific words (dogs and cats). This means that the provision will be applied to other domestic animals, but not to wild animals.

2. Case Law

a) The Rule of Stare Decisis

The second major source of English law are **cases**. In order to find out what the law is in a particular area the judge looks to decided cases rather than statutes or **codes**. Although the number of statutes is increasing steadily, several major areas of law, such as the law of torts and contract law, are still governed to a significant degree by **case law**.

Case law is **inductive**, that means that broad principles are developed from a large number of individual decisions; the judges move from the specific decision to the general rule. In contrast **codified law** is **deductive**; general principles are laid down in advance and are then applied to the individual case.

Decided cases are referred to, and used, to a greater or lesser degree in most legal systems. The difference in the common law is that a previously decided case, a so-called **precedent**

case (or simply **precedent**) is **binding**, it must be followed. This rule is called the **doctrine of precedent** or ***stare decisis*** ('let the decision stand'). There are two main requirements for such a system of precedent. Firstly, there must be a hierarchy of courts. Under the rule of *stare decisis* lower courts must follow the decisions of higher courts and some courts are even bound by their own earlier decisions. It must therefore be clearly discernible from the court system which court is bound by which. The English court system is organised in the form of a pyramid and will be discussed in detail below. Secondly, a reliable system of **case reporting** is necessary, so that judges and lawyers can be sure that the **transcript** of the precedent they are relying on is correct. Case reporting developed privately and rather randomly in the late twelfth and early thirteenth century. The present system, which is much more formal and systematic, developed in the nineteenth century. There are a large number of different **law reports**. The **'Incorporated Council of Law Reporting for England and Wales'**, a non-profit-making organisation, publishes a number of reports, which are checked and, if necessary amended, by judges. For other reports the cases are selected by so-called **reporters** (usually barristers) rather than judges, but they do have the advantage of usually being published sooner. Obviously not all cases which are decided in court can, or need to be reported. Only those cases involving important questions of law will be published; cases involving only questions of fact are not reported.

b) Ratio Decidendi and Obiter Dicta

Not everything a judge says in his judgment is binding on lower courts. What is binding is the so-called ***ratio decidendi***. The *ratio* is the legal principle, the core element of the judgment. It is not always easy to extract the *ratio* from a judgment. Firstly, it can often be interpreted narrowly or widely and the judge in the later case, who is looking to apply the *ratio* of a precedent, then has to decide how it is to be construed. Secondly, the perception of what the *ratio* of a case is may change over time. And finally, it always has to be remembered that, although they do not form part of the *ratio*, the *ratio* is closely linked with the material facts of the case and must always be seen in the light of those circumstances.

Sometimes judges include comments in their judgments that are not strictly necessary for the outcome of the case, for example by stating that their decision would have been the same even if the facts had been different, or by commenting on how the law might develop in the future. Such comments are called ***obiter dicta*** – things said 'by the way'. They have no binding authority, but they may be **persuasive**. This means that lower courts often follow such *obiter dicta*, even though they do not have to. How persuasive a particular *obiter dictum* is depends to a significant degree on the court in which the comment was made. *Obiter dicta* made in the House of Lords, until 2009 the highest court in England, were generally of a high **persuasive authority**.

Obiter dicta are not the only type of persuasive authority. Decisions of the Judicial Committee of the Privy Council, which hears appeals from former colonies and members of the Commonwealth, can also be very persuasive, although they are never binding on English courts. The same is true of cases decided in closely related common law jurisdictions, such as the United States, Canada and Australia. Obviously judgments from other countries will only be persuasive if the law there is similar to English law in the area in question.

c) Distinguishing and Overruling

There are two ways in which a court can decline to follow a precedent which *prima facie* seems to be binding. The judge may come to the conclusion that, although the facts of the case he is dealing with are very similar to those of the precedent, there is a **material** difference between the two. In this case he can **distinguish** the precedent; he declares it to be in some relevant way different from his case, so that the *ratio* of the established case cannot be applied. The difference between the two cases may sometimes appear rather small, but it will always be something material, which clearly distinguishes the precedent from the case at hand. When a case is distinguished it is only declared to be inapplicable to the case the court is dealing with at the moment; it remains binding on all later cases where there is no material difference in the facts.

A judge can also decide that a decision of a lower court should be **overruled** altogether. This means that the earlier case is held by the higher court to have been wrongly decided. Once a case is overruled it is no longer good authority for any later case. Should a judge base his decision on a case that has been overruled, that decision will be reversed on appeal. Generally a court can only overrule the decisions of lower courts, but not its own earlier judgments. The exception is the highest court. The House of Lords gained the right to overrule its own decisions in 1966, and the new Supreme Court will be able to do likewise. However, it is worth noting that the House of Lords was generally reluctant to exercise this power and only did so after careful deliberation.

III. Law of the European Community

In 1973 the United Kingdom became a member of the European Community and passed the **European Communities Act 1972**. Since then **EC law**, the law of the European Community, has become an increasingly important source of law. What distinguishes it from the traditional major sources of English law, case law and statutes, is that it is an external source of law. The European Communities Act states that any United Kingdom Act of Parliament will take effect subject to existing enforceable community rights. This means that EC law takes **precedence** over English law wherever there is a conflict between the two. The constitutional significance of EC membership will be discussed elsewhere. For present purposes it is sufficient to state that EC law can have a binding and direct influence on English law.

IV. Terminology

Blackstone: William Blackstone (1723 –1780) was a prominent academic and judge. His most famous work are the 'Commentaries on the Laws of England'.

By-laws: also called bylaws or bye-laws.

Code: see statute / Act of Parliament.

Coke: Sir Edward Coke (1552 – 1633) is regarded as one of the most eminent jurists in history. His principal work was the 'Institutes of the Laws of England'.

In argument: during the submission made by both sides to the court.

Intra vires / ultra vires: literally 'within the powers' and 'beyond the powers'. These terms are used whenever a person or body has limited powers. A common example of application is company law, where both the company itself and individuals in it are limited in what they can do. Any act which is outside the powers given to, for example, a director, is *ultra vires*.

Law merchant: also referred to as *lex mercatoria*.

Law reports: there are a increasing number of law reports available, ranging from the general to very specific ones. Widely used reports include the All England Law Reports, the Law Reports Appeal Cases, the Law Reports Queen's Bench Division and the Weekly Law Reports. Subject-specific reports include the Lloyd's Law Report and the Industrial Relations Law Report. Law reports must be distinguished from **law reviews** and **journals** (such as the Cambridge Law Journal, the Law Quarterly Review and the Modern Law Review) which contain articles and comments on cases, but not actual transcripts of the decisions.

Material difference: does not necessarily mean big difference; it means that a difference is sufficiently important to be of legal consequence, even if it appears quite small.

Obiter dicta: the term *obiter* can also be used on its own, as in "he said *obiter*" or "in an *obiter* comment".

Precedent: can refer to the doctrine of precedent, or to a particular case which must be followed.

Rules of interpretation: the word 'wife' provides a good example of how the three rules of interpretation work. In many cases the literal rule will be applied, as the word has a clear and unambiguous meaning. Take, however, the following hypothetical situation. A statute provides that 'a bigamist must pay damages to his second wife' (for example for wedding expenses). *Prima facie* the word 'wife' is unambiguous, but in the present context it does not make sense. Under English law a person cannot get legally married if he (or she) is already married to someone else; therefore a woman who marries a bigamist cannot become his wife. The golden rule must be applied to find an interpretation that makes sense. Therefore 'wife' must be interpreted as 'the woman who completed the ceremony of marriage'. The mischief rule can be illustrated by a similar example. A statute might state that the wife of an accused cannot be forced to testify against him. The aim of this could be to exclude people who are in a close and personal relationship with an accused from the duty to testify. However, wives are not the only people in this category, and the court can decide to interpret the term 'wife' widely, so as to include fiancées and girlfriends.

Statute / Act of Parliament: a statute must not be confused with a code. A statute is an individual law, while a code is a systematic collection of laws. Codes are very common in many continental systems (see, for example, the *Bürgerliches Gesetzbuch* and the *Code Napoleon*, the German and French civil codes), but English law is not codified. There are, however, some **codifying statutes**, which bring together in one piece of legislation the common law rules of a particular area of law. An example of this is the Sale of Goods Act 1893 (now the Sale of Goods Act 1979). Continental codes must not be confused with **codes of practice**, which are issued by a wide variety of bodies and organisations. These lay down rules of conduct for a profession or particular actions, but they are not legally binding.

Statutory interpretation: strictly speaking, interpretation of a statute must be distinguished from **construction**. Interpretation simply means that a meaning is given to the words of an Act of Parliament. Construction occurs when ambiguities or uncertainties are resolved. However, the distinction is rather technical and is not often evident, as the correct meaning of a statute will normally only be discussed in court where there is, in fact, uncertainty.

Trade usages: an example is the 'baker's dozen', which is 13 items, instead of the usual 12.

V. Review and Discussion

1. *What is the doctrine of precedent?*

According to the doctrine of precedent, decided cases are binding on subsequent decisions. This means that a lower court must follow the ruling of a higher court. However, not every part of a judgment is binding. The relevant element of a precedent is the *ratio decidendi*, the reason for the decision. Other comments made by the judge, which are not strictly necessary for the decision, are called *obiter dicta* and are not binding. A judge does not have to follow an established case if he can distinguish it from the case he is dealing with, on the basis of a material difference. A higher court can also overrule the decision of a lower court, if it believes it to have been wrongly decided.

2. *What is the relationship between statute law and case law?*

Rules of law are binding, whether they are based on statute or case law. In many areas statutory rules exist side by side with common law principles, for example in contract law, where some issues are covered by an Act of Parliament and others are not. However, if there is a conflict between legislation and case law, the statute prevails. This means that any Act of Parliament overrules cases that are inconsistent with it. The courts cannot refuse to apply a statute. They only have the power to interpret legislation, that is to decide on its precise meaning and application to individual situations.

3. *Evaluate the present day importance of the minor sources of law.*

An increasing number of judgments contain references to and extracts from textbooks. It has become very common for judges to refer to not only old established works of legal scholarship, but also modern publications. Books of authority can therefore be regarded as the most influential minor source of law today. It is interesting to note in this context that there is also an increasing trend to look to other jurisdictions for potential solutions to legal problems.

It is difficult to estimate how often new legal customs are recognised in England, because the cases in question normally deal with questions of fact only and are therefore not reported. However, there is no doubt that new customs can be established even today, which means that they remain a direct source of law.

The principles of the law merchant provide the foundations of modern commercial law and thereby continue to influence the law. However, this influence is only indirect, as the law merchant no longer exists as a separate body of law.

Canon law no longer has any direct influence on modern law, as the ecclesiastical courts are now completely separate from the English courts of law.

4. *Which presumptions operate in relation to statutory interpretation?*

In interpreting Acts of Parliament the courts will make a number of presumptions, *i.e.* it will be assumed that Parliament did not intend to do any of the following, unless there are express provisions to this effect. It should be kept in mind that these presumptions are not irrebuttable, they are only further aids in the process of statutory interpretation.

Presumption against alteration of the law: if Parliament intends to change existing law, it should do so expressly. (It should be remembered, however, that Parliament does frequently alter the law.)

Presumption against imposing liability without fault: in most situations liability will only be imposed on an individual if he was at fault, for example because he acted negligently or intentionally. Parliament should clearly indicate its intention to create an offence where liability is imposed in the absence of any degree of fault.

Presumption against depriving a person of a vested right: the courts will try to protect the existing rights of a person, unless a statute expressly deprives him of one.

Presumption against ousting the courts' jurisdiction: Parliament must use clear and unambiguous words if it intends to restrict an individual's access to the courts.

Presumption that the Crown is not bound by a statute: one of the remaining prerogatives of the Crown is that it is only bound by an Act of Parliament if it is expressly named in it.

5. ***What are the advantages and disadvantages of case law and the doctrine of stare decisis?***

One of the main advantages of the doctrine of *stare decisis* is that it combines certainty with flexibility. Certainty is created by the fact that comparable cases will be decided in the same way; this knowledge allows people to regulate their conduct accordingly. At the same time case law is sufficiently flexible to take account of new situations. As society and technology develop, new situations arise which must be addressed by the law. Changing statute law can be a lengthy process, because of constraints on parliamentary time and the complexities of the legislative process. Case law can be much more easily adapted to accommodate changes and deal with new problems. Furthermore, unlike a code, case law has no limited field of application; there are therefore no areas which cannot be dealt with. Finally, case law is very practical. The courts only decide cases that involve a real dispute, they do not deal with matters that are purely academic or abstract. As a result of this the law has always developed around problems that actually occur; the results reflect the needs of society, rather than being based on a theoretical estimate of potential future problems.

However, case law, and especially the doctrine of precedent also have some disadvantages. The certainty of *stare decisis* can turn into rigidity of the law, as the courts are often reluctant to depart from an established rule. This restraint is not surprising when one considers the inherent conservatism of the system. The courts are always looking back at older cases to establish what the law is. This does not encourage innovative thinking, and it might take some time for judges to realise that a particular rule is no longer adequate. A further danger lies in the fact that a judge may draw illogical distinctions between cases in order to avoid the application of a particular precedent. Cases can be distinguished if there is a material difference between them; if a differentiation is based on lesser grounds, it does not provide a logical basis for future cases. Finally, the sheer bulk of precedent cases can cause problems. The number of reported cases is growing steadily, decisions are inflated by the number of precedents cited and it is becoming increasingly difficult for lawyers to find all relevant cases.

6. ***Explain the following: [1903] 2 K.B. 740; [1932] A.C. 562; [1991] 4 All E.R. 907; [1991] 1 Q.B. 1; [1993] 3 W.L.R. 786; [2003] EWHC 2493; [2002] EWCA Civ 1407; [2005] EWCA Crim 52; [2003] UKHL 62***

The first five examples are **citations** of cases, which set out where they can be found in the law reports. Cases are always cited in the same way and every case can be clearly identified by its citation. The order of citation is: the year in which the case was reported (in square brackets), the volume number (if there is more than one volume for that year), the abbreviation of the report (each report has its own abbreviation) and the page number.

The above citations lead to the following cases (the full names of the reports are given in brackets):

[1903] 2 K.B. 740: *Krell v Henry* (Law Reports King's Bench).

[1932] A.C. 562: *Donoghue v Stevenson* (Law Reports Appeal Cases); the case was actually reported under the name of M'Alister (the claimant's maiden name), but it is generally known as *Donoghue v Stevenson.*

[1991] 4 All E.R. 907: *Alcock and others v Chief Constable of the South Yorkshire Police* (All England Law Reports).

[1991] 1 Q.B. 1: *Williams v Roffey Bros. & Nicholls (Contractors) Ltd* (Law Reports Queen's Bench).

[1993] 3 W.L.R. 786: *Barclays Bank v O'Brien* (Weekly Law Reports).

The King's Bench and the Queen's Bench Report are the same; it is called King's Bench during the reign of a king, and Queen's Bench during the reign of a queen.

Many law reports are now also available on the World Wide Web and on legal databases.

The remaining four examples are so-called **neutral citations**, a system that focuses not on where a case is reported, but on the court in which it was decided. Here the order of citation is: the year in which the case was decided (in square brackets), the abbreviation of the court and the case number (individual to each case).

The above citations lead to the following cases (the full names of the courts are given in brackets):

[2003] EWHC 2493: *Brennan v Bolt Burdon* (High Court of England and Wales).

[2002] EWCA Civ 1407: *Great Peace Shipping Ltd v Tsavliris Salvage (International) Ltd* (Court of Appeal of England and Wales, Civil Division).

[2005] EWCA Crim 52: *R v Coutts* (Court of Appeal of England and Wales, Criminal Division).

[2003] UKHL 62: *Shogun Finance Ltd v Hudson* (United Kingdom House of Lords).

When a case is referenced, both the neutral citation and the case report should be given. The new Supreme Court will have its own neutral citation.

Chapter 4: The Court System

I. Introduction

The English court system is a **two-tier system**, with one branch for **civil cases** and one for **criminal cases**. There are no separate branches for areas such as administrative law and there is no constitutional court. **Civil** and **criminal jurisdiction** are also not completely separated, because most courts deal with both types of cases. The present court system was largely established by the **Judicature Acts 1873-75**, which abolished the old common law courts and transferred their jurisdiction to the new courts. Further reforms were introduced, *inter alia*, by the **Courts Act 1971** and the **Supreme Court Act 1981**. The most significant recent changes have been made by the **Constitutional Reform Act 2005 (CRA 2005)**. It has created a new Supreme Court, which takes over from the House of Lords as the highest court in the country.

The court system is organised in the form of a pyramid. If one party is not satisfied with the ruling of the court it can, in certain circumstances, **lodge** an **appeal** with the next highest court, *i.e.* it can ask the higher court to **review** the decision of the lower court. Magistrates' and county courts, being the most inferior courts, only have **original jurisdiction**; they only deal with cases at **first instance** and do not hear appeals. The next tier of the pyramid are the Crown Court, the High Court of Justice and the Court of Appeal, collectively known as the **Senior Courts** of England and Wales. Crown Court and High Court have both original and **appellate jurisdiction**, so that they can hear cases of first instance and appeals from the lower courts. The Court of Appeal and the Supreme Court, on the other hand, deal exclusively with appeals.

II. The Courts

1. Magistrates' Courts

The **magistrates' courts** have both civil and criminal jurisdiction. On the civil side they deal with the recovery of certain debts, for example payments for water and electricity, and domestic and matrimonial matters. The criminal cases which are dealt with by the magistrates' courts are mostly minor offences, so-called **petty crimes**. In this respect the magistrates' courts are of great practical importance, because the vast majority of crimes which are brought before a court start and end in the magistrates' court. The magistrates' court can impose **fines** or terms of **imprisonment** up to certain limits. All crimes for which the minimum penalty is higher cannot be tried in the magistrates' court.

Cases before the magistrates' courts are usually heard by a panel of three unpaid **lay magistrates**; more complex or sensitive cases are heard by a **district judge**. Magistrates are appointed by the Lord Chancellor on advice of a local committee, while district judges are experienced solicitors and barristers who are appointed by the Lord Chancellor following an application process administered by the Judicial Appointments Commission. Lay magistrates do receive training concerning their duties, but they do not have a legal education as such. They are assisted by the **clerk of the court**, who is himself legally qualified and advises on questions of law, practice and procedure. However, the magistrates do not have to follow his advice, and he must not directly interfere with the decision. In addition to his advisory function the clerk is responsible for the administration of the magistrates' court.

Appeal from the magistrates' courts lies to the High Court in civil matters and to the Crown Court and a Divisional Court of the High Court in criminal cases.

2. County Courts

The **county courts** in their present form were established by the **County Courts Act 1846**. Their jurisdiction is relatively limited in that they deal only with civil cases, and only with smaller claims, the value of which does not exceed certain fixed amounts of money. In addition their jurisdiction is limited geographically in that it is **local**. This means that there must be some connection between the case and the county court before which it is brought. The country is divided into a large number of **districts**, which are grouped into **circuits**. Normally an action will be brought either at the **place of residence** or **place of business** of the defendant, or in the district where the events which lead to the action occurred.

County courts are **presided** over by **circuit judges**. They are assisted by **district judges**, who supervise the administration of the courts and exercise limited **judicial authority**. Each circuit judge may sit in several county courts and, if necessary, may move between **circuits**.

Appeal from the county court lies to the Court of Appeal, except for bankruptcy matters, which go to a Divisional Court of the High Court.

3. Crown Court

Unlike magistrates' and county courts, which are separate courts spread all over the country, the **Crown Court** is just one court, which can sit anywhere in the country at any time, and even in several different places at the same time. When sitting in London the Crown Court retains its historical name of **Central Criminal Court** and is colloquially referred to as the **'Old Bailey'**, after the street in which the court building is situated.

The jurisdiction of the Crown Court is exclusively criminal. It deals with all criminal cases that are not heard before the magistrates' courts (usually the more serious ones). It also has jurisdiction to hear appeals from decisions in the magistrates' courts. Should a defendant plead 'not guilty' to the offence he is being charged with, the trial will be conducted before a judge and a jury consisting of twelve lay members of the public.

The judges of the Crown Court are **High Court judges**, circuit judges and **recorders**, who are experienced solicitors and barristers acting as part-time judges. The offences which are dealt with in the Crown Court are divided into four **classes**, depending on their nature and gravity. The more serious offences have to be tried before a High Court judge while the less serious ones are dealt with by circuit judges and recorders.

From the Crown Court appeal lies both to a Divisional Court of the High Court and the Court of Appeal (Criminal Division). Where the defendant was acquitted, *i.e.* found not guilty, by the Crown Court, the Attorney-General may refer any point of law that was raised in this case to the Court of Appeal for a decision, if he feels that the issue is so important as to make a full discussion of it desirable. This is the so-called **Attorney-General's Reference**. The Court of Appeal may likewise refer the case to the Supreme Court. The acquittal of the defendant is not affected by the decision of the Court of Appeal or the Supreme Court.

4. High Court of Justice

Like the Crown Court the **High Court** is one court which may sit anywhere in England or Wales. It consists of three **divisions** (Queen's Bench Division, Chancery Division and Family Division) and has both civil and criminal, and original and appellate jurisdiction.

It is staffed by High Court or **puisne judges** who are divided between the three divisions.

From all divisions of the High Court appeal lies to the Court of Appeal. In certain circumstances an appeal directly to the Supreme Court may be possible, under the so-called **leapfrog procedure**. Criminal matters also progress directly to the Supreme Court.

a) The Queen's Bench Division

The **Queen's Bench** Division is headed by its **President** and is the largest division of the High Court. The main work of this division is as a court of first instance for civil matters, especially contract and tort claims. The specialist **Admiralty Court**, **Commercial Court** and **Technology and Construction Court** are also part of the Queen's Bench Division.

The division can hear appeals in civil matters, for example from certain **tribunals**, but most appeals are criminal appeals from the magistrates' courts and the Crown Court. This jurisdiction represents the entire criminal jurisdiction of the High Court and it is appellate only. The appeals are dealt with by a **Divisional Court**, which consists of two or three judges of the division.

Supervisory jurisdiction is an important third type of jurisdiction exercised by a Divisional Court of the Queen's Bench Division. By using so-called **prerogative orders** it can control inferior courts, tribunals and other public bodies with a judicial or quasi-judicial function and can compel them to exercise their powers correctly.

b) The Chancery Division

The **Chancery Division** is presided over by the **Chancellor of the High Court**. Its original jurisdiction covers those matters which were dealt with by the Court of Chancery prior to its abolition in 1873, including, *inter alia*, matters relating to land, mortgages, trusts, the administration of **estates** of deceased persons and bankruptcy. Other areas, such as landlord and tenant disputes, have been added by statute. The Chancery Division also includes a specialist court, namely the **Patent Court**, which deals with patent actions.

The Chancery Division is mainly a court of first instance. However, it does have a limited appellate jurisdiction, for example in relation to bankruptcy cases, which are heard by a Divisional Court of the Chancery Division.

c) The Family Division

The **Family Division** is headed by its **President** and, in effect, deals with all cases concerning matrimonial issues and children which come before the High Court. Such cases include matters relating to legitimacy and adoption and certain proceedings under statutes like the **Family Law Act 1986** and the **Children Act 1989**.

In these matters the Family Division has both original and appellate jurisdiction. The appeals it deals with mainly come from the magistrates' courts.

5. Court of Appeal

Although the **Court of Appeal** can sit anywhere in the country it almost exclusively sits in London. It consists of a Civil and a Criminal Division and its jurisdiction is appellate.

The judges of the Court of Appeal are called **Lords Justices of Appeal.** In addition High Court judges may be requested to sit in either division. The Lords Justices of Appeal normally sit in **panels** of three, unless a case is considered to be very important, in which case a **full court** of five judges may sit. Each Lord Justice may deliver his own judgment; the appeal is decided by the majority.

The decisions of the Court of Appeal are binding on all lower courts and on the Court of Appeal itself. Appeal from decisions of both divisions lies to the Supreme Court.

a) The Civil Division

The **Civil Division** is headed by the **Master of the Rolls (MR)**. It hears appeals on **points of fact and law** from the High Court and the county courts and from a number of tribunals, such as the **Employment Appeal Tribunal.**

In virtually all civil cases an appeal to the Court of Appeal is only possible if **permission to appeal** has been granted. Permission will be refused if a case has no realistic prospect of success. The Civil Division can **allow** or **dismiss** the entire appeal, or it can allow one part of an appeal and dismiss the other.

b) The Criminal Division

The President of the **Criminal Division** is the **Lord Chief Justice** (LCJ). It deals with appeals from the Crown Court. There are different possible **grounds for appeal.** Appeals on a point of law are always possible. Appeals on any other grounds (not involving a point of law) and **appeals against sentence** can only be brought with **leave,** *i.e.* permission, of the Court of Appeal.

The Criminal Division can dismiss the appeal, or allow it and **quash** the conviction in question. The Court of Appeal is generally very reluctant to admit new evidence, but it may do so if the new evidence is material, and can then order a new trial.

6. The Supreme Court and the House of Lords

Until 2009 the House of Lords was the highest court of appeal for England and Wales. Under the CRA 2005 its powers and jurisdiction have now been transferred to the new independent **Supreme Court,** which opens on 1 October 2009. This represents a significant constitutional change, and it remains to be seen how it will affect the operation of the court in the future. The Supreme Court is the first court in the UK that will allow some proceedings to be filmed and broadcast.

For hundreds of years the House of Lords had combined political and judicial functions, acting both as one of the two chambers of Parliament and the highest court in the country for civil and criminal matters. Its judicial functions, which are of historic origin, were however exercised solely by the **Appellate Committee of the House of Lords,** consisting of the **Lords of Appeal in Ordinary** (the so-called **Law Lords**). The overlap between the functions was therefore more limited in reality than it appeared, especially as the Law Lords very rarely particiapted in political debates. Nevertheless, it was felt that a clearer separation of powers was needed. Unlike the House of Lords, which sat in the Palace of Westminster, the Supreme Court has its own building opposite the Houses of Parliament.

The former Law Lords are now the twelve **Justices of the Supreme Court**; the senior Law Lord has become the **President of the Supreme Court**. Law Lords originally appointed to the House of Lords will retain their titles, but will no longer be entitled to participate in debates and votes in the House of Lords. New Justices will be appointed directly to the Supreme Court and will not be given peerages.

In the House of Lords, cases were usually heard by five Law Lords, with the most important cases being heard by nine. Each Law Lord delivered his own judgment, called **opinion**, and the case was decided by the majority. Often not all Law Lords would prepare a full opinion, but would simply express their agreement with the reasons given by one of the others – unless, of course, they disgreed, in which case they would deliver a **dissenting opinion**. It is expected that the procedure in the Supreme Court will be similiar.

The Supreme Court is the highest court of appeal for both civil and criminal matters, as well as dealing with devolution issues which previously fell within the remit of the Privy Council. It will only hear cases that raise **arguable points of general public importance**. Appeals will normally come from the Court of Appeal, but in certain circumstances an appeal directly from the High Court is possible under a procedure called **leapfrogging**. A party must always obtain permission to appeal. Decisions of the Supreme Court, like those of the House of Lords, are binding on all lower courts.

7. Privy Council

Like previously the House of Lords the **Privy Council** has a dual function. It is the last remnant of the *Curia Regis*, the early advisory body of the king. Its members are mainly former and present cabinet ministers and the Lords of Appeal in Ordinary; it is lead by the **Lord President of the Council**. Today its role is mainly advisory and formal, although it does have a limited power of issuing delegated legislation by way of **Orders in Council**.

The Privy Council hears certain specialist appeals, for example from the ecclesiastical courts of the Church of England. Under the Constitutional Reform Act 2005 its jurisdiction over devolutional matters has been transferred to the new Supreme Court, but the Privy Council will remain the highest court of appeal for British colonies and a number of members of the Commonwealth. The number of countries which submit appeals to the Privy Council has declined steadily, but countries like Jamaica and Barbados (who still have the Queen as their Head of State) continue to do so.

The decisions of the Privy Council are based on the law of the country which has submitted the appeal and are binding on all courts in that country, but not on English courts. Likewise the Privy Council is not bound by decisions of the English courts. However, decisions of the Privy Council usually have a strong persuasive authority and are often followed in English cases.

III. Simplified Diagram of the Current Court Structure

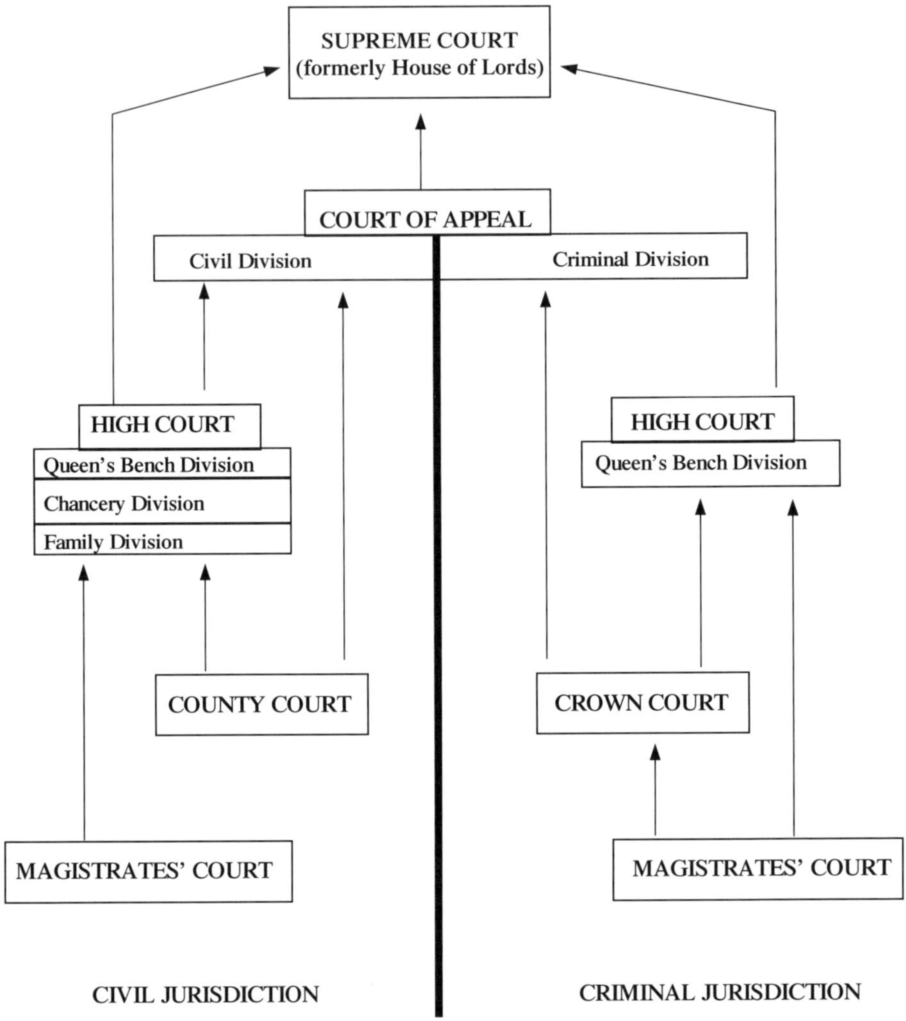

IV. Terminology

Appeal: where a person is not satisfied with the judgment of a court, he can ask a higher court to re-examine the decision. The party making the appeal is called **appellant**, the other party is the **respondent**. It may also happen that both parties wish to appeal (for example, one party because he has been ordered to pay damages, and the other because he thinks the damages awarded are too low). This is known as **cross-appeals**.

Appeal against sentence: a person who has been found guilty can appeal against the sentence imposed by the court, for example if he believes it to be excessive. The fact that he has been found guilty is not affected by this appeal.

Appeal on point of fact / on point of law: a point of fact is an issue which can be determined by evidence. Facts are usually determined in the court of first instance, and appeals on point of fact are limited. The higher appeal courts do not normally interfere with a lower court's finding of fact; they concern themselves with appeals on point of law only.

Divisional Court: must not be confused with the divisions of the High Court. Divisional Courts consist of two or three judges and were created to hear matters that could not be dealt with by one judge sitting alone. Each division of the High Court (the Queen's Bench Division, the Chancery Division and the Family Division) has its own Divisional Court.

Employment Appeal Tribunal: hears appeals from employment tribunals on matters such as unfair dismissals, redundancy payments and sex discrimination.

Estate: the word has several meanings. It can refer to a piece of land or to various types of ownership that exist in relation to property (especially land). In the present context it is used in the wider sense of 'property'. The estate of a deceased person is all the assets that belonged to him at the time of his death.

Lay magistrate: a **lay person** is someone who is not a professional; therefore lay magistrates, unlike district judges, do not have a legal education.

Permission to appeal: the Civil Procedure Rules 1998 changed the terminology for civil cases from 'leave to appeal' to 'permission to appeal'. The terminology in criminal cases remains unchanged.

Puisne judges: pronounced like 'puny'.

Queen's Bench Division: is called **King's Bench Division** when the ruling monarch is a king.

Tribunal: a body which exercises judicial or quasi-judicial functions outside the normal hierarchy of courts. Tribunals usually comprise both lawyers and lay persons with expert knowledge, and have been set up in a number of different (often very technical) areas; **employment tribunals**, for example, deal with employment disputes. The main advantages of tribunals compared to the courts are that the proceedings are cheaper and speedier (for example, parties before a tribunal often appear without legal representation), and that tribunals have more specialist knowledge.

V. Review and Discussion

1. *How does a civil case progress through the court system?*

A limited number of civil matters, especially matrimonial and domestic matters, start in the magistrates' courts. The majority of cases are divided between the county courts and the High Court. The jurisdiction of these two courts overlaps to a certain extent, but generally it can be said that smaller claims are dealt with by the county courts, while disputes which involve more complex issues or greater sums of money are taken to the High Court. Cases which began in the magistrates' courts and the county courts can be appealed to the High Court; from the High Court appeal lies to the Civil Division of the Court of Appeal and from there to the Supreme Court. In certain cases an appeal can go directly from the High Court to the Supreme Court under the so-called leapfrog procedure.

2. How does a criminal case progress through the court system?

Criminal cases start either in the magistrates' courts or the Crown Court; the choice of court depends on the classification of the offence in question. From the magistrates' courts appeal lies to both the Crown Court and the Queen's Bench Division of the High Court. In relation to some issues appeals from the Crown Court go to the Queen's Bench Division of the High Court, but most cases proceed to the Criminal Division of the Court of Appeal and then to the Supreme Court. Cases which are taken to the High Court go from there to the Supreme Court, without going to the Court of Appeal.

3. What are the judges in the different courts currently called?

Magistrates' court: lay magistrates, district judges.

County court: circuit judges, district judges.

Crown Court: High Court judges, circuit judges, recorders.

High Court: High Court or puisne judges. The Queen's Bench Division and the Family Division are headed by their respective Presidents, the Chancery Division by the Chancellor.

Court of Appeal: Lords Justices of Appeal. The Civil Division is headed by the Master of the Rolls, the Criminal Division by the Lord Chief Justice.

Supreme Court: Justices of the Supreme Court, headed by the President of the Supreme Court.

4. What are the differences between civil and criminal cases?

	Case Brought By:	**Nature of Action:**	**Outcome:**	**Aim of action:**
CIVIL CASE	claimant	defendant is sued	defendant liable or not liable	compensation of claimant
CRIMINAL CASE	prosecution (state)	defendant is prosecuted	defendant guilty or not guilty	punishment of defendant

There is also a difference in the citation of civil and criminal cases. *Donoghue v Stevenson* ([1932] A.C. 562) is a civil case. The first name (Donoghue) is the name of the claimant, the second name (Stevenson) is that of the defendant. The 'v' stands for **'versus'** (against), but in civil cases this is spoken as 'and'. This case is thus correctly referred to as *Donoghue **and** Stevenson*.

R v Collins ([1972] 2 All E.R. 1105) is a criminal case. The 'R' stands for **'Regina'** (the Queen; during the reign of a King it represents 'Rex') and is spoken as **'the Crown'**. This shows that the case is brought by the state as prosecutor. The name (Collins) is that of the defendant. In criminal cases the 'v' is spoken as **'against'**, so that the correct reference to this case is *The Crown **against** Collins*.

5. How are criminal offences classified?

Criminal jurisdiction is divided between the magistrates' courts and the Crown Court. More serious offences are tried before a judge and jury in the Crown Court. This mode of trial is called **trial on indictment**. Lesser charges are dealt with by magistrates in a **summary trial**. All offences fall within one of three classifications, which determines in which court the trial will be conducted. Offences which must be brought before the Crown Court are called **indictable offences**. This category includes crimes like murder, manslaughter and rape. Commmon assault, a number of road traffic offences and lesser cases of criminal damage are examples of **summary offences**, *i.e.* they can be tried only by a magistrates' court. The third category comprises crimes which can be dealt with either in the Crown Court or the magistrates' court; they are called **offences triable either way**. Examples include theft and arson. The accused can decide whether to opt for trial by a judge and jury in the Crown Court, or for summary trial before a magistrate.

6. What is alternative dispute resolution?

In recent years methods of resolving disputes without resorting to litigation have become increasingly popular. They have in common that they are based on the involvement of an independent third party and are collectively known as **alternative dispute resolution** or **ADR**. The aim is to avoid the cost, delay and acrimony involved in a court trial.

Arbitration is the most formalised form of ADR, in that it remains basically adversarial. The parties present their case to an **arbitrator**, who is bound to apply the law. However, the procedure is less rigid than before a court and the arbitrator can conduct the matter in the way he regards as most efficient. The decision of the arbitrator, called the **award**, is binding on the parties, but can be appealed to the High Court.

Two other important forms of ADR are **mediation** and **conciliation**. The distinction between these terms is not always clearly drawn, and they are in fact often used interchangeably. They have in common that an agreement is reached by the parties themselves, with the help of a neutral third party, rather than being imposed by a judge or arbitrator. This outcome is not binding on the parties. The third party will try to help the parties identify the issues and find solutions which are acceptable to both sides. The main advantage of this form of ADR is that it enables the parties to maintain a good working relationship, basing a solution on reconciliation rather than adjudication. The difference between mediation and conciliation lies in the degree of involvement of the third party. The job of a **mediator** is to help the parties identify their own solutions; he is in effect assisting in the negotiations. A **conciliator** will take a more active part in the process by suggesting possible solutions; thus he might act more like an arbitrator whose decisions are not binding.

Chapter 5: Trial System

I. The Adversarial System

The term **'adversarial system'** refers to the way in which litigation is conducted before the court. The origins of this system can be found in the historical concept of trial by battle, which was introduced into England by the Normans. In the adversarial system the two parties to a dispute are regarded as equally matched opponents who 'fight' before the court, while the judge acts as an independent umpire. He remains largely passive, listening to the evidence presented to him and usually interfering only to clarify an obscure point. The judge does not undertake his own investigations. This means that the full responsibility for the preparation and submission of the case lies with the parties. They have to ensure that all relevant information is presented to the court, and is presented well. The emphasis is very much placed on oral evidence, so that the performance of the lawyer can have a significant influence on the outcome of the case.

The adversarial system can be contrasted with the **inquisitorial system** used in many continental countries. There the judge takes a much more active part in the proceedings and the process of investigation. Critics of the adversarial system usually point out that in many cases the parties are not actually equally matched, for example where an individual faces a large company.

At this point it should be noted that, while the distinction between adversarial and inquisitorial system is a convenient shorthand for referring to the differences in the way in which trials are conducted, it is an oversimplification. Firstly, parties before a court are always in an adversarial position, and the judge is always an independent arbiter, not an inquisitor in the true sense of the word. Secondly, and more importantly, reforms introduced by the Civil Procedure Rules 1998 have increased the involvement of the court in all stages of the proceedings. Judges now have much more influence over how a case is prepared and presented and are therefore no longer completely passive. Various rules compel the parties to co-operate more (especially during the pre-trial stage), although of course their basic positions as opponents remain unchanged.

II. The Jury

1. Origins of the Jury System

There is a long tradition of **jury trial** in England, with the earliest forms probably existing even before the Norman Conquest. Over time two different kinds of juries developed. On the one hand there was the **grand jury**, which consisted of up to 24 members. Its function was to decide what offence a person should be charged with, and to present the accused to the royal judges for trial. These duties were gradually taken over by the justices of the peace, and by the time the grand jury was abolished in 1948 it had long become a mere formality. The second kind of jury was the **petty jury** of 12 persons. This is the true ancestor of the modern jury. From the thirteenth century on trial by jury began to replace the traditional trial by ordeal. The members of the jury were in effect witnesses, chosen because of their intimate knowledge of the locality and the parties involved. Gradually their role changed, and by the early sixteenth century members of the jury were selected for exactly the opposite reason, namely because they were not personally connected with the case.

2. Composition of the Jury

A modern **jury** is a group of 12 persons, randomly selected from society to decide questions of fact in civil and criminal cases. The members of the jury are called **jurors**. They are selected at random from the electoral register by the **Jury Central Summoning Bureau (JCSB)**, the body responsible for the **summoning** of jurors. The number of potential jurors summoned will depend on the number of cases to be tried. The names are then entered on lists, called **panels**. The actual jury for each case is then selected from the panel for the court in question.

Generally every person who is between 18 and 70, is registered on the electoral register and has been ordinarily resident in the United Kingdom for at least five years since the age of 13, can be chosen for **jury service**. There are, however, several categories of people who are either not allowed or not obliged to **sit on** a jury.

People suffering from a mental illness and those convicted of certain criminal offences are **disqualified** from jury service. The detailed rules include, for example, those who have been sentenced to life imprisonment (who are permanently disqualified), and those who have served a prison sentence in the last ten years (whose disqualification is temporary). **Ineligibility** also used to cover individuals involved in the administration of justice (such as barristers, solicitors, police officers and judges) as well as members of the clergy, but this was changed by the entry into force of the **Criminal Justice Act 2003**, and membership of a particular profession or vocation no longer excludes an individual from jury service.

Excusal as of right is available for those who have served on a jury within the previous two years. This means they can be jurors if they want to, but must be excused if they so request. Members of Parliament, members of the armed forces serving abroad and medical personnel used to have an automatic right to be excused, but this was again removed by the Criminal Justice Act 2003.

Discretionary excusal permits the JCSB to excuse a person who is otherwise eligible to serve on a jury from doing so. The JCSB must be convinced that there is a 'good reason' for a citizen to be excused from jury service, such as a medical condition. Instead of excusing someone from jury service entirely the JCSB has the power to **defer** when an individual will have to serve as a juror. Deferral can be granted for the same reasons as a discretionary excusal and the JCSB operates on the basis that it is always the preferred option. A reason to grant a deferral may, for example, be that a holiday has already been booked and paid for.

Jurors receive compensation for loss of earnings, travelling expenses and similar expenditure, but they are not paid for sitting on a jury.

3. Challenging of Jurors and Jury Vetting

Prosecution and defence have the right to **challenge** any juror **for cause**. This means that they can ask the judge to remove a particular person from the jury, provided that there is a good reason for doing so, for example because a juror is illiterate.

The prosecution can also ask a juror to **'stand by for the Crown'**. The juror who has been asked to **stand by** does just that – he stands to one side. If there are sufficient other potential jurors left on the panel, the juror in question will not serve. If the panel has been exhausted the prosecution must show cause to prevent the juror from sitting on the jury. In theory stand-by is only a form of provisional challenge, not a challenge without cause, as the investigation into cause is only delayed. In practice, however, the prosecution rarely has to prove that a good reason for challenging a juror exists, because there are normally sufficient alternative jurors present. The right of stand-by is therefore potentially open to abuse, as the prosecution could use it to influence the composition of the jury. In order to avoid this, the Attorney-General has issued guidelines, which lay down that the right of stand-by should not be used to gain a tactical advantage, but only to exclude someone who is manifestly unsuitable.

As was seen above the members of the jury are selected at random, and there are only a limited number of grounds for exclusion. Obviously it must be possible to check a potential juror's criminal record, in order to establish whether he is disqualified. Any checks into the background of individuals which go beyond this, for example by investigating their occupation or political opinion, are known as **jury vetting**. After it became publicly known that jury vetting had taken place (always in favour of the prosecution) in several high-profile cases, the Attorney-General made it clear that such checks are only allowed in very exceptional circumstances. Jury vetting may be allowed in cases which involve national security, where part of the evidence is likely to be heard **in private** (*i.e.* not in open court), and in terrorist cases. In security cases there is a danger that a juror may be susceptible to pressure, which could lead him to disclose evidence given in private, while in terrorist cases political beliefs might be so biased (for example in relation to Northern Ireland) that a fair and impartial trial would not be possible. Any such checks must be authorised by the Attorney-General; they are then called **authorised checks**.

4. Use of thc Jury

Generally, juries can be used in both civil and criminal cases. However, the use of civil juries has declined markedly over the last few decades and most civil cases are now heard by a judge sitting alone. The right to trial by jury has been limited to four specific cases, namely actions for fraud, defamation, malicious prosecution and false imprisonment. In all other civil cases the judge has a discretion to allow trial by jury. According to guidelines laid down by the Court of Appeal the discretion should only be exercised in exceptional circumstances; in practice a jury trial is indeed granted only rarely. Even in those cases where a right to trial by jury still exists the case may be heard by a judge alone, if he is of the opinion that the case is unsuited for trial by jury, for example because it involves complicated documents which would have to be scrutinised, or complex scientific evidence. Where a jury is used the jurors decide whether the defendant is liable or not, and what amount of damages, if any, he has to pay.

Where cases are decided by individual judges rather than 12 ordinary members of the public, the outcome is generally regarded as more predictable and more uniform, especially as far as the award of damages is concerned. One of the major criticisms of civil juries is that damages awarded by them are often exorbitant and bear little relation to the loss actually suffered. This is especially true in defamation cases, where juries have frequently awarded previously unprecedented amounts of damages.

Criminal juries are still a well-established part of the English legal system. There is no jury in the magistrates' courts, but cases before the Crown Court are heard by a jury, which determines the question of guilt. If the defendant is found guilty the judge fixes the sentence. Should the accused plead guilty to the charges the jury does not get involved; the judge simply decides on the sentence.

The right of an accused to be tried by a jury of his peers is regarded by many as a cornerstone of the criminal justice system in England and Wales. However, the administration of justice also requires that jurors understand the facts in issue and the evidence relied on by all parties. In recent years the use of juries in complex fraud trials has been questioned and the Criminal Justice Act 2003 contains provisions to allow such trials, which often involve difficult and technical evidence, to be heard by a judge alone. In 2006 the Government tried to amend the relevant section so as to automatically remove juries in such cases, but this attempt was abandoned after it met fierce resistance in the House of Lords.

In addition, the Act allows for criminal trials to be conducted without a jury on application by the prosecution at the start or during trial. For a court case to take place or continue without a jury there must be a real danger of **jury tampering**, that could not be overcome by any other measure. The first such application was granted in June 2009.

5. The Role of the Jury

The purpose of trial by jury is to involve society as a whole in the judicial process, by letting randomly selected members of the general public decide questions of fact in a court of law. This is thought to strengthen the legitimacy of the legal system by ensuring that not all power is placed in the hands of professionals.

The role of the jury during the trial is passive; the jurors sit in the **jury box** and listen to the evidence as presented by both sides and to the **summing-up** of the judge. In this summing-up the judge reminds the jury of the vital issues of fact and law involved in the case. He will inform them, for example, about the **burden** and **standard of proof** and the elements of the offence in question, and will remind them of the evidence they have heard.

The jury then retires to the **jury room** to deliberate and discuss the case. Once the jury has reached a decision it returns to the court room and the **foreman** of the jury (who has been selected by the members of the jury themselves to announce the result) presents the **verdict**. Generally the decision of the jury must be **unanimous**, but a **majority verdict of** 11:1 or 10:2 is acceptable, if the judge has stated that he will accept such a verdict. If the jury fail to agree on an outcome and the trial judge does not accept a majority verdict, the case is declared a mis-trial. The jurors are discharged, and the case may be retried before a newly-selected jury.

One important aspect of the work of juries is the concept of **jury secrecy**. This means that the discussions which take place in the jury room must be kept absolutely secret. Members of the jury are not allowed to disclose, nor are outsiders allowed to enquire after, the opinions and votes of individual jurors; it is a contempt of court to do so. One aim of this rule is to protect jurors from outside pressure and harassment by ensuring that no outsider knows the details of the deliberations. In addition, it encourages jurors to speak openly and frankly during the discussions.

Historically a person tried and acquitted of a criminal charge could not be tried again for that same offence; this is known as the rule against **double jeopardy**. In some limited circumstances this rule has been removed by the Criminal Justice Act 2003. For certain qualifying offences, such as homicide and serious sexual offences, a second trial of someone already acquitted may be possible, where new and compelling evidence exists.

III. Terminology

Burden of proof: obligation of a party to legal proceedings to prove a particular fact (or facts). The general rule is that the party who asserts that something is true must prove that it is. Thus the burden of proof is usually on the claimant (in civil cases) or the prosecution (in criminal cases); it can, however, shift to the defendant in certain circumstances.

Jury tampering: interference with members of a jury by intimidation, bribery or other persuasive means.

Majority verdict: does not mean a simple majority; in order to be valid as a majority verdict, the decision of the jury must be taken 11:1 or 10:2. A split of, for example, 7:5 is not sufficient.

Standard of proof: the degree of proof that is required to establish the truth of a particular fact. In civil cases, the relevant standard of proof is **'on a balance of probabilities'**, while in criminal cases a fact must be proven **'beyond reasonable doubt'**.

Summing-up: summary of the evidence by the judge to the jury. Must be distinguished from a **direction** to the jury: the judge instructs the jury on any questions of law (he tells them what the law is), so that they can apply points of law to the facts of the case. Directions on points of law will usually be included in the summing-up.

Unanimous verdict: where all members of the jury are in agreement as to whether a defendant is guilty or not guilty.

Verdict: the decision of the jury on a question of fact presented to them in a civil or criminal trial. The verdict must be distinguished from a judgment, which is the formal decision of a court (*i.e.* one or several judges).

IV. Review and Discussion

1. *What are the main features of the English trial system?*

One of the main features of the English trial system is the adversarial style of litigation. The parties are responsible for presenting their case; the judge remains largely passive and will normally only intervene to clarify an obscure point. Emphasis is placed on the oral presentation of evidence. It should be noted, however, that under the current rules governing civil procedure, the judge takes a much more active part in the preparation and presentation of cases, thus reducing the adversarial nature of the process (although it is, of course, not eliminated).

The second main feature is trial by jury, where questions of fact are determined by a jury of 12 randomly selected members of society. While this mode of trial is now used only rarely in civil cases, and a (perhaps surprisingly) small number of criminal cases, it is regarded by many as a fundamental guarantee of fair trial.

2. *What is jury vetting? Is it allowed in England?*

The term 'jury vetting' refers to the practice of conducting checks on the backgrounds of potential jurors which go beyond checking for criminal records. The aim of such checks was to collect information (for example on occupation, financial situation and political background) in order to predict how an individual might vote in a case. The prosecution could then exclude jurors which they thought were likely to decide in favour of the defendant. Jury vetting is not allowed in English law. Only in very limited circumstances will the Attorney-General permit so-called authorised checks.

3. What are the advantages and disadvantages of trial by jury?

The jury system allows ordinary members of society to participate in the administration of justice; the verdict is seen as coming from society rather than an individual judge. This can help to maintain public confidence in the judicial system. Juries are also seen as the prime safeguard against abuse of judicial or prerogative power, especially in criminal cases. The jurors are free to decide a case according to their conscience. This means that they can acquit a defendant if they think it is right to do so, even if he has clearly committed an offence. This usually happens where a case involves a morally or politically controversial subject, or where prosecutions brought by the government are regarded as oppressive. A well-known example is the case of Clive Ponting. Mr. Ponting was a civil servant, who passed confidential information on to a journalist, revealing that the government of the day had lied to Parliament. Disclosing this material was a clear breach of the **Official Secrets Act**, which prohibits the disclosure of information relating to national security; nevertheless the jury refused to convict.

However, the use of juries also creates some problems. Jurors can be intimidated or threatened (such behaviour is known as 'jury nobbling'). They may lack objectivity through being subconsciously prejudiced, or may simply be unable to understand the evidence, for example in complex fraud cases. This can leave them susceptible to the persuasive influence of counsel. The quantum of damages awarded by juries (especially in defamation cases) is often excessive and bears no relation to the loss actually suffered by the claimant. Finally, juries do not give reasons for their verdict, which can make it difficult for the parties involved to identify possible grounds for appeal.

4. How is the verdict of the jury phrased in a criminal and civil case respectively?

In a criminal case the jury will find the defendant "guilty" or "not guilty" of each offence that he is charged with. In a civil case the jury will find the defendant "liable" or "not liable".

Chapter 6: Legal Personnel

I. Judges

1. Appointment

Unlike in some continental countries, being a **judge** in England is not a completely distinct legal career, as members of the **bench** (as judges are referred to collectively) are selected from among practising lawyers. There is also no fixed system of promotion. A judge does not have to start his career in the lower courts; he can enter the profession higher up the judicial ladder.

Judicial appointments are another area affected by the Constitutional Reform Act 2005. Under the old system, judges were appointed by the Queen on the advice of the Lord Chancellor or Prime Minister. Now, the new independent **Judicial Appointments Commission** (**JAC**) plays a key role. The Commission is composed of a lay chairmen and 14 commissioners, who are judges, legal practitioners, lay justices and non-lawyers.

For judicial appointments up to and including High Court judges (but excluding magistrates), the JAC selects candidates on merit following an open application procedure, and recommends these to the Lord Chancellor. The Lord Chancellor can accept or reject the recommendation made to him, or ask the Commission to reconsider, but he cannot chose an alternative candidate. A selected candidate is formally appointed by the Queen. Magistrates continue to be appointed by the Lord Chancellor on advice of a local committee.

For appointments to the Court of Appeal and to the posts of Lord Chief Justice and the Heads of the Divisions of the High Court the JAC convenes separate selection panels, whose membership depends on the appointment to be made. In each case, the panel makes a recommendation which the Lord Chancellor can accept, reject or ask to be reconsidered.

The selection panel for appointment to the Supreme Court is convened by the Lord Chancellor. The formal appointment for all senior posts is once again made by the Queen.

In the past, only barristers could become judges. In 1990 appointment to the bench became dependent on the candidate's **right of audience**, *i.e.* the right to appear before a court as an **advocate**. As solicitors can now have a right of audience in all courts, they became eligible for judicial office (the first former solicitor was appointed to the House of Lords in 2009). Under the new rules, solicitors and barristers must have held the relevant legal qualification for five to seven years, and must have gained legal experience during that time. They are encouraged to work as part-time judges before applying for a full-time position.

2. Tenure

The **Act of Settlement 1700** laid down that as long as judges conducted themselves properly (*quamdiu se bene gesserint*) they could only be **removed** by an **address** to the Queen by both Houses of Parliament, and no longer by the will of the King. This rule, known as **security of tenure**, still applies to judges of the High Court and above. Other judges and magistrates, however, may be removed by the Lord Chancellor for incapacity or misbehaviour. Recorders may also be removed for failure to comply with the conditions of appointment (relating, for example, to the duration of the appointment or the availability of the individual recorder). The normal retiring age for judges is 70, although an extension until 75 may be granted in exceptional cases.

3. Judicial Independence

Judges must be completely **independent** once they are in office. An important part of the work of the courts is the scrutiny of executive actions through judicial review, and this can only be done effectively by an independent judiciary.

The security of tenure granted to judges plays an important part in maintaining this independence, because judges need not fear that they might be removed if they, for example, decide that a minister has acted unlawfully. A second important element of this independence is the principle of **judicial immunity**. Judges may not be sued in relation to acts done within their jurisdiction. The immunity of the judges of the superior courts is therefore almost complete, because their jurisdiction is unlimited. Circuit judges and recorders are only immune while they remain within their (much more limited) jurisdiction. Generally speaking, judges may not be sued in defamation for anything said in court, and this immunity extends to statements made by others in court, such as the parties or witnesses. Likewise, an action for false imprisonment may not be brought against a judge in respect of any sentence of imprisonment imposed by him.

II. Legal Professions

In England the **legal profession** is divided into two distinct branches, namely **solicitors** and **barristers**. Although the term **'lawyer'** can be used to refer to either one or the other it is very important to maintain the distinction, because there are significant differences both in the training and the work of solicitors and barristers.

1. Solicitors

a) Education and Training

Most people who intend to become a solicitor will start by taking a three-year **law degree** at university. However, this is not an essential prerequisite. Graduates of other degrees can qualify for the **vocational training** for solicitors by passing the **Common Professional Examination** (CPE) or the **Postgraduate Diploma in Law** (PgDL). Vocational training starts with a one-year full-time course called the **Legal Practice Course** (LPC). While the law degree will have provided the academic background, the LPC deals with the practical aspects of the work of a solicitor, for example how to draft a legal document. After having passed the final exams, the prospective solicitor will undertake a two-year **traineeship** with a **firm of solicitors**. In order to be able to do this a student must obtain a **training contract** with the firm in which he intends to complete his training. Many (though not all) training contracts will include a kind of sponsorship, in that the solicitors agree to pay the (very substantial) LPC fees for the student. During the two years the **trainee** will normally work in a number of different departments, so that he becomes acquainted with all the different aspects of a solicitor's work. Once a trainee has finished his training contract he will be admitted as a fully **qualified solicitor**.

b) Work

The work of a solicitor is very diverse, both in relation to the kind of work undertaken, ranging from preliminary advice to advocacy, and the subject-matter, which can include subjects as diverse as contract law, family and matrimonial matters and crime. Solicitors can work on their own, in **partnerships**, or in **Limited Liability Partnerships** (LLPs).

A large part of the work of a solicitor consists of the drafting of legal documents, such as wills and contracts, and dealing with property matters like conveyances and mortgages. The solicitor is also the first person someone with a legal problem will approach. He will give advice and, if a matter is to be taken to court, he will start the action by filing the required documents. The solicitor will also deal with all other preparatory stages of litigation, such as the interviewing of witnesses and the preparation of evidence.

Whether or not a solicitor can represent his client in court depends on whether he has a right of audience. Solicitors traditionally had a right of audience before the lower courts, namely the magistrates' and the county courts. This has been extended significantly and they can now appear in all courts up to the High Court, provided that they have completed a special course in advocacy skills, called the **Professional Skills Course**, during their training contract. Solicitors with a certain length of advocacy experience can take further exams on matters such as evidence and procedure and can thereby qualify as **solicitor advocates**; this gives them a right of audience up to and including the Supreme Court (formerly the House of Lords). In those cases where the solicitor cannot or does not wish to go before a court himself, he must hand the case over to a barrister.

c) The Solicitors Regulation Authority and the Law Society

Until 2007 the **Law Society** was the governing body of solicitors. It was responsible for professional training through the Legal Practice Course, decided which courses a university must offer as compulsory elements of its law degree so that graduates can directly enter the LPC and set out **rules of conduct**. These regulatory and disciplinary matters (such as dealing with allegations of **misconduct** against a solicitor) are now the responsibility of the independent **Solicitors Regulation Authority**. The Law Society remains important as the representative organisation of the profession, for which it provides a range of services.

2. Barristers

a) Education and Training

The first step of the training of a barrister is the same as for solicitors, in that he must either have a law degree, or must pass the CPE or PgDL. The prospective barrister must then be admitted by one of the four **Inns of Court**, namely **Gray's Inn**, **Lincoln's Inn**, **Inner Temple** and **Middle Temple**. The Inns originated as living quarters for advocates and have survived until today as the professional organisations of the **Bar**. Although their jurisdiction is not statutory, they have very important disciplinary powers. They are solely responsible for the **calling of barristers** and the admission of students. After having been accepted by one of the Inns the prospective barrister must complete a one-year vocational course, called **Bar Vocational Course** (BVC), and pass the **Bar Final Examination**. He must also keep a certain number of **'terms'** in his Inn, which he does by dining there on a number of occasions per term. He will then be **'called to the Bar'** by his Inn. Before he can practice as a barrister, however, the student must serve a year of **pupillage**, during which he will follow, and learn from, a senior member of the Bar. After completing pupillage, a barristers becomes a member of chambers by being offered **tenancy**.

b) Work

The main part of the work of a barrister is **advocacy**, the presenting of cases before court. He has a right of audience before all courts in England, up to and including the Supreme Court (formerly the House of Lords) and the Privy Council. When acting before a court he is also referred to as **counsel**. Barristers can either be self-employed and work in sets of **chambers**, or employed as in-house legal counsel by firms and organisations. Barristers that work in chambers essentially work for themselves, but share the administrative costs of operating a legal practice, such as renting premises and paying **clerks'** wages.

Generally a self-employed barrister does not have direct contact with his client, but receives instructions from a solicitor, who is said to **brief counsel**. This used to be the only way that a barrister could undertake work, but steps to modernise the profession and widen access to legal experts have encouraged the establishment of **Licensed Access** and **Public Access**. These programmes allow organisations and members of the public to approach certain barristers directly.

Barristers usually specialise in a particular field of law, and the solicitor will chose the barrister he feels is most suited for representing his client. A barrister must accept a case offered to him, unless he would not be able to provide his best services to the client because of other engagements; this is known as the **'cab-rank' rule**.

The most experienced and able barristers may be appointed as **Queen's Counsel** (QC) on the recommendation of the **Independent Selection Panel**. A barrister can apply for such a recommendation after at least ten years at the Bar. If he is appointed he is said to **'take silk'**, as the **robes** of QCs are made of silk. (Traditional **gowns** and **wigs** are still worn before many courts, though some changes have recently been introduced.) QCs usually deal with the more complex or important cases.

c) The Bar Standards Board and the Bar Council

Like the Law Society, the **Bar Council** used to combine regulatory and representative functions as the governing body of the Bar. In 2006 the two were separated with the creation of the independent **Bar Standards Board**, which regulates entry to the Bar and sets standards of professional practice. The Bar Council remains the profession's central body for all other matters.

III. Law Officers

The **Attorney-General** (A-G) and his deputy, the **Solicitor-General**, are the so-called **law officers**.

The Attorney-General has both political and legal duties. He is a member of the government and gives legal advice to government departments. He represents the Crown in certain civil cases and in actions for treason or similarly politically or constitutionally sensitive crimes. The Attorney-General can also enter a so-called ***nolle prosequi*** in criminal cases. This is a prerogative power which halts the prosecution in question, and may be exercised if, for example, it is in the public interest that the prosecution is not continued. An important part of the work of the Attorney-General are **relator actions.** In these proceedings he appears on behalf of the general public, or a section thereof. In effect he is acting as a guardian of the public interest in cases such as public nuisance, where an action cannot be brought by an individual. Although the Attorney-General is the head of the English Bar, he may not engage in private practice while in office.

The Solicitor-General is the deputy of the Attorney-General. Despite his title he is a qualified barrister, not a solicitor, and may also not engage in private practice while in office. He may act on behalf of the Attorney-General if authorised to do so by the Attorney-General, if the Attorney-General is ill or if the post of Attorney-General is vacant.

IV. Crown Prosecution Service

The **Crown Prosecution Service** (**CPS**) was established by the **Prosecution of Offences Act 1985**, which created the first national system for the prosecution of offences independent of the police. The head of the Crown Prosecution Service is the **Director of Public Prosecutions** (**DPP**). In complex cases, or those of public interest, the DPP will take over the **prosecution process** from the police. It should be noted that the CPS does not control the process of **investigation**. Investigations are carried out by the police and the information is then passed on to the Crown Prosecution Service. Crown Prosecutors have a limited right of audience; where they cannot appear before court themselves they must instruct a barrister.

V. Terminology

Bar: the English Bar is the professional body of barristers; the term can also be used to refer to the profession of barrister itself. The name is derived from a partition across a court of justice, which separates the bench and counsels' seats from the rest of the court. Qualified barristers are invited to approach this bar to address the court.

Bench: literally, the seat of a judge in court. Someone appointed as a judge is said to have been **raised to the bench**.

'Cab-rank' rule: this term literally refers to the rule that where taxis are waiting (for example outside a train station), the first in line must take the first passenger that approaches; the driver cannot refuse to drive someone a short distance in the hope of securing a more lucrative fare.

Common Professional Examination: a one-year course which covers the English legal system, the seven core subjects (contract law, criminal law, equity and trusts, European law, property law, public law, tort law) and legal research skills. Although the term CPE is still used, it is increasingly referred to as the Postgraduate Diploma in Law.

Firm of solicitors: solicitors often work together in partnerships, which are usually referred to as firms. Some firms consist of only two partners, while some of the biggest may have hundreds of partners.

Independent Selection Panel: the body set up specifically for the appointment of QCs. It includes lawyers, lay people and a retired senior judge.

Licensed Access: this scheme provides for professionals and organisations to be awarded a licence permitting them to instruct a barrister without the intervention of a solicitor. Organisations wishing to enjoy this right must apply to the Bar Council for a licence.

Limited Liability Partnerships: unlike traditional partnerships, this form of partnership has a separate legal personality to the individuals that are partners of the company. This means that the LPP, and not the partners, is responsible for the debts of the partnership.

Postgraduate Diploma in Law: the course is the same as the CPE, but the name PgDL is becoming increasingly popular.

Public Access: barristers that have been in practice for at least three years and have been approved by the Bar Council can be approached directly by members of the public to provide legal advice and representation. The public may only approach a barrister in this way in connection with civil matters, for criminal and family matters a solicitor must still brief counsel.

Tenancy: at the end of pupillage a barrister will need to become a member of chambers in order to practice. The relationship between barristers and the chambers is called a tenancy, because it developed from (and is still based on) the hire of rooms: the barrister makes a financial contribution to the upkeep of chambers which allows him to operate his practice from that location.

Vocational training: training relating to a particular employment or occupation.

VI. Review and Discussion

1. *What is the relationship between security of tenure, judicial immunity and judicial independence?*

Security of tenure means that judges cannot be removed from office unless they are guilty of misconduct. They are therefore not vulnerable to political pressure or similar influences. Judges are also immune from suit in relation to acts done within their judicial capacity. Nothing which transpires in a court of law can be the subject of a personal action against the judge. Judicial immunity and security of tenure are granted to ensure that judges are completely independent while in office. This enables them to base their judgments exclusively on the law, without having to worry about potential personal consequences of unpopular decisions. The need for this independence is especially obvious in cases involving judicial review. The effectiveness of this form of control of executive actions would be severely affected if judges were subject to political pressure.

2. *What are the main differences between solicitors and barristers?*

The professions of solicitor and barrister differ both in relation to their training and the work they undertake. Prospective solicitors begin by taking the LPC and then complete their vocational training in a firm of solicitors, under a two-year training contract. Vocational training for barristers consists of the BVC and one year of pupillage. Each profession also has its own representative body, the Law Society and the Bar Council, and its own regulatory authority, the Solicitors Regulation Authority and the Bar Standards Board. As regards business structures, solicitors are usually employed by a firm, while most barristers are self-employed. Legal work used to be clearly divided between solicitors and barristers. The former were responsible for dealing with and giving advice to clients, drafting legal documents and completing the preparatory stages of court actions, while the latter presented the cases in court. (Solicitors could only appear in front of magistrates' and county courts.) The distinction can no longer be so easily drawn. The right of audience of solicitors has been extended to the High Court, and those qualified as solicitor advocates can appear in all courts, including the Supreme Court (formerly the House of Lords). Advocacy is therefore no longer the exclusive territory of barristers. However, many solicitors continue to hand more complicated cases over to baristers. As regards direct contact with clients, barristers may now chose to accept **instrucions** directly from clients under the new access schemes, but as this is not compulsory, the traditional distinction between the professions remains largely intact.

3. How are judges referred to? How are they addressed in court?

	referred to as:	**written as:**
HIGH COURT	Mr. Justice Smith Mrs. Justice Smith	Smith J. Smith J.
COURT OF APPEAL	Lord Justice Smith Lady Justice Smith	Smith L.J. Smith L.J.
SUPREME COURT	Lord Smith of Solihull Lady Smith of Solihull	Lord Smith of Solihull Lady Smith of Solihull

The first woman to be appointed to the Court of Appeal was referred to as 'Lord Justice' for a significant time, until the address was officially changed to 'Lady Justice'. Judges from the High Court upward are addressed as "My Lord" or "My Lady"; judges in lower courts are addressed as "Your Honour". Magistrates are addressed as "Sir" or "Ma'am" respectively. At present all Justices of the Supreme Court still have titles, so the form of address has not changed. It is not yet known what the correct form of address will be when the first Justice who is not a Lord or Lady is appointed.

4. What are the advantages and disadvantages of the way legal personnel is structured?

The structure of the legal professions has attracted a number of criticisms over recent years. The split between solicitors and barristers means that in many cases a client will have to employ two lawyers in relation to one case – a seemingly unnecessary waste of expenditure. Furthermore, cases could be dealt with more efficiently if one person was responsible from beginning to end, rather than a solicitor handing over to a barrister at a crucial moment. On the other hand, the differentiation between, roughly speaking, advice and advocacy, does have some advantages. In the adversarial system of England, the outcome of an action can depend to a significant degree on the quality of counsel. It is therefore important for the client that his case is presented by a skilled advocate. The present system allows both barristers and solicitors to focus on one particular aspect of legal work, thus enabling them to become experts through specialisation. It remains true that in many cases the expertise of a barrister is not necessary for the presentation of a case in court. This problem has been addressed by the reforms which extended solicitors' rights of audience, as a much larger number of cases can now be both prepared and presented by solicitors.

The main advantage of recruiting judges from among practising lawyers (instead of judicial office being a completely separate career) is that they are already very experienced when they are called to the bench. They know how the trial system works, and are therefore less likely to be influenced by the methods of persuasion used by counsel.

One of the main problems faced by the legal professions today is that they are regarded as elitist and non-representative of society. Women and members of ethnic minorities are underrepresented in all fields of legal work, especially among the judiciary. Judges are traditionally regarded as being male, white and from an upper or upper middle class background, educated at public school and Oxford or Cambridge. (It should be noted that, despite their name, public schools are in fact private schools, most of which charge very substantial tuition fees.) This is reflected in the fact that the first woman was not appointed to the House of Lords until 2004. Efforts are being made to recruit more women and ethnic minorities into the legal professions, but it might be some time before true equality is achieved.

Chapter 7: Pre-trial Civil Procedure

I. Introduction

Pre-trial procedure in civil cases (with the exception of insolvency and family proceedings) is governed by the **Civil Procedure Rules 1998 (CPR)**. Their over-riding objective is to ensure that cases are dealt with justly. In order to achieve this, matters like the complexity of the issues and the amount of money involved influence the way in which a case is handled. The courts are supposed to ensure that the parties are on an equal footing and that actions are resolved quickly and fairly.

The CPR are supplemented by **Practice Directions**, which contain practical guidance as to how the rules contained in the CPR are to be implemented.

II. Case Management

Under the CPR ultimate responsibility for the way in which litigation is handled lies no longer with the parties, but with the court. Judges are expected to engage in active **case management** by giving **directions** as to how the case is to proceed. Emphasis is placed on the early identification of the key issues, so that the parties can not pursue every point regardless of time and expense. Judges also set timetables for the completion of preparatory steps and can limit the evidence the parties can adduce to support their case. While the position of the parties remains adversarial, a certain degree of co-operation is required of them, and the courts actively encourage the use of alternative dispute resolution and **settlements**.

The CPR provide for a number of sanctions, should a party fail to comply with any case management orders. The court can, for example, debar that party from presenting evidence in a particular form or from a particular witness, or it can take the party's behaviour into account when deciding **costs**. If deemed necessary, the court can also strike out a part or even the entire case.

III. Management Tracks

1. Introduction

After proceedings have been initiated by the parties, each case is allocated to one of three **management tracks**: the small claims track, the fast track and the multitrack. The aim is to ensure that each matter is dealt with in the way that is most appropriate. It is up to the court to decide which track is most suitable for a given action. In doing so it must have regard to the nature, financial value and complexity of the issues involved. The parties are required to provide the relevant information by filling in **allocation questionnaires**. Once the court has decided which track the case should be allocated to, it informs the parties by way of a **notice of allocation**.

2. Small Claims Track

The **small claims track** is designed for cases with a financial value of up to £5,000. The aim is to deal with smaller disputes in a relatively informal and therefore less time-consuming manner. Various procedural rules, such as the rules on disclosure, do not apply to the small claims track and parties are encouraged to appear without legal representation. The right to appeal is limited to situations in which there was a serious irregularity in the proceedings or the court made a mistake of law.

The court will normally give **standard directions** to the parties. These will set out that the parties must serve copies of any documents on which they intend to rely and must bring the originals to the hearing. The parties will also be informed of the date and duration of the hearing. If these standard directions are inappropriate, for example because some issues require clarification, the court can also give **special directions**.

3. Fast Track

The majority of defended actions with a financial value between £5,000 and £25,000 will be allocated to the **fast track**, as will many non-monetary claims, *i.e.* claims for remedies such as injunctions and specific performance. Once a case is assigned to this track the court will give directions ordering the parties to disclose documents and serve witness statements and expert reports, and informing them of the timetable they must follow. The directions will also set a trial date no more than 30 weeks later. Alternatively, the court can fix a **trial window**, a period of up to three weeks during which the trial will take place. This relatively short period between the start of proceedings and the trial is the salient feature of the fast track (hence the name). Failure to comply with the **directions timetable** can lead to sanctions being imposed on the defaulting party, but the date of the trial will not normally be postponed.

4. Multi-Track

Generally speaking, the **multi-track** will cover all cases which are not allocated to the small claims track or the fast track. It is therefore the track for cases with a value exceeding £25,000 and most substantial High Court actions. Obviously the multi-track has to deal with a wide variety of cases and the courts will have to adopt a very flexible approach. It is therefore not easy to make general statements about procedure on this track.

As with the other tracks the court will give directions as to how the case is to proceed and set the trial date or period. This may be sufficient for a straightforward case, but more complicated actions will require more detailed case management. The CPR therefore provide for case management conferences, listing questionnaires and pretrial reviews. A **case management conference** gives the court the opportunity to ensure that the key issues of the dispute are identified. **Listing questionnaires** are used to check that the parties have complied with earlier directions and provide up-to-date information that helps the court to decide on the timetable for further pre-trial proceedings. The court has a further opportunity to assess the parties' compliance with directions at the **pre-trial review**. This hearing is also a good chance to promote settlement between the parties.

IV. Initiating Proceedings

1. Initiating a Claim

Every case is initiated by the **claimant**, the person who wishes to bring an action, against the **defendant**, the person against whom an action is brought. The claimant fills in a **claim form**, in which he must give details of the court in which he wants to bring the action and of the parties involved. He must also provide a concise statement of the nature of his claim, what remedy he is seeking and, if he is claiming money, what the value of the claim is.

This claim form must then be **served** on the defendant. **Service** can be effected in several ways, including personal service, **first class post** and fax or other form of electronic communication. This applies to all documents that must be served by either party to the other during the course of proceedings.

The claimant must also provide the defendant with the **particulars of claim**, which can be included in the claim form or served separately. In the particulars of claim he must, *inter alia*, summarise the facts on which the claim is based, state whether he is claiming aggravated or exemplary damages (and if so, the grounds on which they are claimed) and give details of any allegation of fraud or misrepresentation. If the claim is based on a written agreement, a copy of the contract should also be included. The particulars of claim may also contain reference to any point of law on which the claim is based, and the name of any witness the claimant intends to call at the trial.

2. Responding to a Claim

The defendant need not do anything until he has received the particulars of claim. Once this document has been served on him, he can chose between three possible responses. If he admits that the claimant's claim is justified, he can **file** an **admission**. Judgment will then simply be entered for the claimant, who will receive the remedy he has asked for on the claim form. The defendant disputes the claim by filing a **defence**, stating the reasons why he denies the allegations made by the claimant. He can also set out his own account of events, if this differs from the claimant's. If the defendant wishes to defend the action, but is unable to file a defence within the time limit (for example because relevant information is not available to him), he can file an **acknowledgement of service**.

Rather than just defend the claim made against him, the defendant may wish to bring his own action against the claimant. This crossaction is known as a **counterclaim**. It is filed with the defence and is treated as if it were a claim. The relevant information should therefore be set out in the same format and detail as is required of particulars of claim.

The claimant can respond to any issues raised in the defendant's defence in a **reply**. However, he is not obliged to do so, and failure to file a reply is not to be taken as admission of any allegation made in the defence. In contrast, the defendant is taken to admit any allegation made by the claimant which he does not specifically deny. The reply can be followed by the claimant's defence against the counterclaim.

3. Statement of Truth

As can be seen from the above, there are various documents in which the parties formally set out their case: claim form, particulars of claim, defence (and counter-claim) and reply (and defence to counterclaim). These documents are collectively referred to as **statements of case**. Every statement of case must be verified by a **statement of truth**. This is a statement to the effect that the party putting forward the document believes that the facts stated in it are true. The statement must be signed by the party in question or his legal representative. To sign a statement of truth without an honest belief in the truth of the document is a **contempt of court**.

V. Disclosure

In practically all cases the court will give directions that each party should provide the other with information on which his claim is based. The formal procedure for the exchange of **documents** is called **disclosure**. A party discloses documents by stating that they exist or have existed. It should be noted that disclosure is only the process of revealing the existence of a document; actually making the document available to the other party is covered by the separate rules on **inspection**.

Standard disclosure requires each party to disclose all documents on which he relies, as well as documents which adversely affect his own or another party's case, or support another party's case. The duty is limited to documents which are or have been in that party's control. Each side must make a reasonable search for documents that fall within one of the above categories. What is 'reasonable' will depend on a variety of factors, such as the number of documents involved, the nature and complexity of the proceedings and the significance of any document that is likely to be located during the search.

The court can also order **specific disclosure**, for example by ordering a party to disclose a particular document, or to carry out a particular search and disclose all documents discovered as a result.

VI. Evidence

The parties will try to prove the disputed facts by placing **evidence** before the court. The principle of case management enables the court to control this process to a significant degree. The court can limit the number of **lay** and **expert witnesses** each party may call. Directions will be given ordering each party to serve **witness statements**, that is written documents which contain the evidence provided by a witness, which the party intends to rely on at trial. The court can also decide on which issues it actually requires evidence, and how it is to be provided. In exercising these powers the court can even exclude evidence which would otherwise be admissible.

VII. Judgment Without Trial

1. Default Judgment

The defendant must respond to the claimant's claim within a certain time of receiving the particulars of claim. If he fails to file a defence or acknowledgement of service, the claimant can enter **judgment in default.** This means that the court will give judgment without the case being tried. The procedure for obtaining a **default judgement** depends on the nature of the claim. A simple **request-for-judgment procedure** is available in money claims. The claimant request that judgment be entered for him, and the court grants judgment without considering the merits of the claim. In other cases the claimant must make an application to the court, which will consider the case at a hearing and will decide what the claimant is entitled to on the basis of his statement of case.

A default judgment can be **set aside** if it was entered wrongly, or if it appears to the court that the defendant has a real prospect of successfully defending the claim.

2. Summary Judgment

After the defendant has filed an acknowledgement of service or defence, either party can apply to the court for a **summary judgment**, *i.e.* for judgment without trial. The application must be made by way of an **application notice**, and must be supported by evidence. Summary judgment will be granted if the court is of the opinion that the **respondent** has no real prospect of success. Thus, if an application is made by the claimant, summary judgment will be entered if he can show that the defendant has no defence to the claim; if the application is made by the defendant, he must show that the claimant has no real prospect of winning.

VIII. Legal Aid

Under the system of **legal aid** the Government provides funding for those who cannot otherwise afford to pay for legal advice or representation. The system is administered by the **Legal Services Commission** (**LSC**) and offers different kinds of financial assistance via a network of contracted providers. Legal aid is available for all stages of proceedings. A solicitor can provide preliminary advice and prepare a case for court (called **Legal Help**), or he can speak on the client's behalf in a hearing (called **Help at Court**). At its most extensive, legal aid will cover the cost of full **Legal Representation** during a trial, but this will only be granted if the LSC considers it reasonable (taking into account, for example, the applicant's chances of success).

All legal aid is subject to a strict **means test**. Applicants must provide information about their income and any existing capital to show that they are **financially eligible**. One of the main criticisms of the present system is that the financial limits are far too stringent and exclude many people who cannot afford to become involved in legal proceedings; in addition, legal aid is not available for all types of cases.

IX. Terminology

Contempt of court: a criminal offence, punishable by imprisonment. A person will be in contempt if he in some way obstructs the course of justice, or shows disrespect for the court's authority. A party to proceedings may also be guilty of a contempt of court by failing to comply with an order made by the judge.

Costs: the expense incurred through a party's involvement in an action, such as solicitors' fees. Often the unsuccessful party will be ordered to pay his opponent's costs, as well as his own.

Directions: in the directions the judge sets out how a case is to proceed, *i.e.* what the parties have to do, and when. These directions must not be confused with the Practice Directions that supplement the CPR. The Practice Directions contain different standard forms, including standard directions, which courts can use or modify to suit the facts of the individual case.

Document: defined as anything in which information of any description is recorded (this includes disks, audio and video cassettes, computer programmes etc.).

First class post: in England, mail can be sent either by first or second class post. First class is more expensive, but faster than second class.

Legal Services Commission: the central body responsible for providing and regulating the public funding of legal proceedings in England and Wales.

Respondent: the party making an application is called the **applicant**, the other party is called the respondent.

Setting aside: a judgment which is set aside is cancelled.

Settlement: a voluntary agreement by the parties to end civil litigation before the case is tried. The parties can **settle out of court** at any time and without having to observe any formalities.

X. Review and Discussion

1. *What are the main objectives of the CPR? How are they achieved?*

The rules on civil procedure embodied in the CPR are aimed at streamlining the way in which civil cases are dealt with by the courts. In order to make the process as quick, cheap and fair as possible judges take an active part in the pre-trial process. The key word is case management. Judicial participation ranges from ensuring that the parties limit themselves to the important issues and complete preparatory steps within a reasonable time, to actively encouraging the parties to settle. Courts also benefit from increased flexibility in the way they handle cases, which allows them to adopt the procedure that is most suited to the circumstances of the individual dispute (taking into account matters such as the complexity of the issues involved and the financial value of the claim).

2. *What are the salient features of the three management tracks?*

The small claims track is intended for cases involving relatively small amounts of money. The aim is to keep proceedings simple and straightforward, to avoid unnecessary complication of the issues. To this end a number of procedural rules do not apply, which makes it easier for parties to represent themselves.

Claims with a higher financial value and those aimed at non-monetary remedies are the domain of the fast track. Emphasis is placed on the expeditious resolution of disputes. There will normally be a strict timetable for the completion of the pre-trial stage and the trial date will be set within a certain maximum period after the commencement of the action.

The multi-track will deal with all cases not assigned to one of the other management tracks (usually claims involving greater sums of money). The procedure is very flexible, to take account of the diversity of cases which fall under this heading. The judge is given several opportunities to collect information and to ensure that the parties have complied with his directions. This enables him to decide which procedure is best suited to an individual claim.

3. *Explain the terms 'conditional fees' and 'pre-action protocol'.*

The solicitor of a successful client will receive any money that the unsuccessful opponent is ordered to pay as costs. In addition, solicitor and client can enter into a **conditional fee agreement**, which provides that in the event of the claimant's victory in court the solicitor will be paid an additional sum out of the damages awarded. This **success fee** is calculated as an agreed percentage of the costs awarded and can be up to 100 percent (although it is usually a lower figure). Thus, in the event of success, the solicitor will receive up to double the amount of remuneration; if the case is lost he will receive nothing. Conditional fees must be distinguished from **contingency fees**, which are common in the USA, but unlawful in England. Under a contingency fee agreement the lawyer of a successful client receives an agreed percentage of the total amount of damages awarded; the difference is that, while conditional fees are paid out of damages recovered, they are calculated as a percentage of the amount of costs awarded.

Pre-action protocols are documents, approved in Practice Directions, which set out how the parties are supposed to act prior to the commencement of litigation. The **Pre-action Protocol for Personal Injury Claims**, for example, sets out a standard letter that a solicitor should send to a proposed defendant, to ensure that he is informed of all relevant facts, and lists potentially pertinent documents, so that each side can go through the list and identify those that might be relevant in their case. The aim is to promote the early and fair settlement of cases by establishing contact between the two sides and improving the exchange of information. Even if settlement cannot be achieved, the parties will be well-informed at the outset of the pre-trial process, thus avoiding unnecessary delay. The pre-action protocols are not binding as such, but any failure to comply can be taken into account by the judge when he gives case management directions and makes orders for costs.

4. What is a Part 36 Payment?

A **Part 36 Payment,** formerly called a **payment into court** is, in effect, a formalised offer to settle the claim. The defendant pays a sum of money that he regards as satisfaction for the claim to an officer of the court. The claimant can decide whether to accept the sum offered or not. If he accepts, the dispute is resolved; if he rejects the offer the case is tried in the normal way. The court is not informed of the fact that a payment has been made, so this cannot affect the outcome of the case. If, at the end of the trial, the claimant is awarded an amount of damages that is lower than, or equal to, the defendant's offer, or if the ruling is in some other way less favourable for him, he will normally have to pay the other side's costs from the time the payment was made. The reason for this is that the claimant did not gain anything by refusing the offer; he has prolonged the process unnecessarily, and should therefore compensate the other party for the expense incurred during that time. The claimant can also make a Part 36 Payment, by informing the defendant of the amount of money that he would be prepared to accept in settlement of his claim. If the defendant accepts this offer, the case is settled; if the offer is rejected and the claimant is eventually awarded a higher sum in damages, the defendant must pay the claimant's extra costs.

Chapter 8: Constitutional Law

I. Nature of the Constitution

1. The Unwritten Constitution

Most countries recognise that, in addition to the 'normal' law, there are fundamental principles according to which the country is governed. Often these rules are regarded as a higher form of law and are embodied in a single document, called the **constitution.** **Great Britain** is very different in this respect, because it does not have a **written constitution.** There are several documents, such as the Magna Carta of 1215 and the **Bill of Rights** of 1689 which contain important principles, but there is no single document (or a group of documents) which sets out 'the constitution'. The reasons for this are mainly historical. Many of the most famous written constitutions were drafted when the countries in question were making a fresh start and wanted to show a clean break with the past. Examples include the American Constitution which marked the step from colonial rule to independence and the German *'Grundgesetz'* which was drafted as a result of defeat in war. The history of Britain, however, has for a long time been marked by continuous development rather than dramatic change, so that a 'fresh start' like that experienced by Germany and the United States of America never took place.

So Britain does not have a written constitution. This does not mean, however, that it does not have a constitution at all. As will be seen below a significant number of constitutional principles are recognised and adhered to in Britain. The fundamental difference between Britain and most other countries is not that Britain does not have a constitution, the difference is that the British constitution is **unwritten.**

Sources of constitutional law can be divided into **legal** (case law and statutes) and **non-legal** sources (conventions).

2. Constitutional Conventions

An important source of **constitutional law** are **constitutional conventions**. Some of the most important principles of government are based on conventions, or non-binding rules. There is no law that there must be a Prime Minister, or how the Prime Minister is to be chosen, yet there always is a Prime Minister, and he is always chosen in the same way. Conventions are not contained in Acts of Parliament or judicial decisions and are therefore not enforced by the courts. Nevertheless they are always followed by those to whom they apply. One reason for this is that it is simply a lot easier to follow established conventions, rather than face the political problems which a deviation from existing principles would cause. One of the main advantages of conventions is that they can more easily change over time and can therefore be adapted to suit changes in practice. This means that the constitution is much more flexible than one which is contained in a written document.

II. Important Constitutional Principles

1. The Rule of Law

The **rule of law** is perhaps the most difficult element of constitutional law. Although people are often quick to protest that something is "against the rule of law", few have a clear idea of what this concept actually entails. The reason is that it can be – and has been – interpreted in about as many different ways as there have been legal theorists. In the present context, no attempt will be made to emulate the likes of Aristotle and **Dicey**, who have been instrumental in developing the meaning of the rule of law. The following is only intended to outline some of the most commonly accepted elements of this principle.

At the centre of the rule of law lies the belief that all men, including those who govern, are subject to the law, no-one is above it. "Law" in this context refers to a higher form of natural justice, which all man-made rules must comply with. This supremacy of the law leads to the recognition of several maxims, most of which set out procedural limits for the legal system. Thus it is generally accepted that the law must be sufficiently certain, so that people can know in advance what legal consequences might be attached to a particular action. Closely linked with this is the principle of non-retroactivity, which is regarded as particularly important whenever an individual's liberty or other important rights are at stake. Furthermore, all acts done by ministers or other officials must be authorised by law, and all discretionary powers should be subject to safeguards against their abuse. In addition to these essentially formal elements, recent commentators have emphasised the substantive aspects of the doctrine, such as the existence of an independent judiciary, equal access to justice and the prohibition of unfair discrimination.

The above are just some of the interpretations of the rule of law. Despite the obvious difficulties that stem from its indeterminate nature, the rule of law is a key element of constitutional law, and its power to restrict governmental authority and protect the rights of individuals should not be underestimated.

2. The Royal Prerogative

The **royal prerogative** today is the sum of those unique legal powers which remain vested in the **Crown** and no-one else (*i.e.* which have not been abolished by statute). The prerogative consists of a number of **powers, rights, privileges** and **immunities**. However, the term **prerogative powers** is normally used to indicate all the above. Some prerogative powers are exercised by the Queen personally, while others are exercised by the government of the day on behalf of the Crown. The prerogative derives from the common law; therefore new prerogative powers cannot be created by statute. Established ones can, however, be abolished by an Act of Parliament. The courts have traditionally been very reluctant to interfere with the exercise of the royal prerogative. They would determine whether a particular prerogative existed, but once its existence had been established the courts would not interfere with the way the power was exercised. However, in recent years their reticence has somewhat lessened, provided that the content and subject-matter of the prerogative in question are justiciable.

The royal prerogative includes the following powers and immunities. The Queen **summons** and **dissolves** Parliament and gives Royal Assent to statutes. Under the **prerogative of pardon** the Crown may pardon convicted offenders (this power is exercised only on advice of the Home Secretary). Some prerogative rights are of less practical importance, like certain proprietary rights which exist in relation to sturgeon, whales and swans. The inherent rights of the Crown can also be exercised in respect of the external relationships of the country, as the making of treaties and the declaration of war and peace are also covered by the prerogative. Immunities include the personal immunity of the Queen from being sued and the immunity from income tax liability.

3. Parliamentary Sovereignty

The concept of **Parliamentary sovereignty** originated in the seventeenth century when Parliament began to erode the powers of the King. Since then this principle, also referred to as **Parliamentary supremacy**, has become one of the most important doctrines of constitutional law. According to this concept Parliament can make or unmake any law on any issue – no matter how harsh, unfair or nonsensical a statute may be. Thus Parliament could decide that all cars should be painted green, or that all people should walk backwards. Because Parliament is **sovereign** English courts cannot question the **validity** of an Act of Parliament (provided that the correct procedure has been followed). This is an important difference between England and many other countries which have special constitutional courts to ensure that statutes do not conflict with the constitution. There is no such court in the English legal system. If there is a conflict between the common law and statute law (or even between a constitutional principle, such as the rule of law and statute law), the latter will always prevail.

Parliamentary sovereignty also means that Parliament cannot bind its successors. Any Act which is passed by one Parliament can be repealed later by the same or a different Parliament. This application of Parliamentary sovereignty is especially important when issues like fundamental human rights are being discussed. Many constitutions, such as the German one, provide for the **entrenchment** of those provisions they regard as particularly important. This means that such provisions can only be changed if a certain majority of votes is obtained and sometimes clauses are even expressed to be completely unchangeable. In 1998 the English Parliament passed the Human Rights Act, which brought parts of the European Convention on Human Rights into national law. However, these provisions are not entrenched in any way; Parliament cannot protect them from being repealed at a later date like any other statute.

A question which has caused much debate in recent decades is whether Parliament lost any or all of its sovereignty when the United Kingdom became a member of the European Community. The two basic positions are as follows. Some people argue that because directly applicable measures of EC law automatically become part of the law of each Member State, Parliament has indeed surrendered its supremacy in all areas to which EC law applies. The counter-argument is that the European Communities Act 1972, which effected the UK's accession to the EC, could be repealed at any time in the future just like any other statute, which would restore full sovereignty to Parliament. The loss of power is therefore regarded as at most temporary.

As Parliament is the highest legislative authority there are no legal limitations on its ability to make law. This does not mean, however, that Parliament can in practice do whatever it wants. There are a number of restrictions which, although they are not legal in nature, can be very effective in controlling what Parliament does. Public opinion is one such factor. The government (which strongly influences legislation) will normally be wary of introducing legislation which would be very unpopular (especially when general elections are approaching) or which is opposed, not by the public as a whole, but by a powerful pressure group. Likewise there would be little point in passing an Act of Parliament which could not be enforced in practice. The government also has to ensure that international obligations are fulfilled and will try to avoid measures which would lead to international condemnation.

4. The Doctrine of Separation of Powers

The doctrine of **separation of powers** is a constitutional principle which can be found in many different constitutions across the world. The main elements of this doctrine can be described as follows. The functions of government are divided into three distinct categories, namely the **legislative**, the **executive** and the **judicial**. These functions should be carried out by three corresponding organs of government, the **Legislature**, the **Executive** and the **Judiciary**. If one organ exercises more than one class of function, individual liberty is threatened.

There is a clear distinction in England between the three organs of the state. The government is the executive, Parliament is the legislature and the courts are the judiciary. However, until recently there were some significant inroads into the separation of powers. One example are the Law Lords who, until summer 2009, were both judges of the highest court in the country and full members of the House of Lords as the Upper House of Parliament. They could therefore exercise both judicial and legislative functions. This has now been changed with the creation of the Supreme Court, whose judges will no longer sit in the House of Lords. (It is worth noting that even when the Law Lords were able to participate in political debates they very rarely did so, ensuring that the separation of powers was greater in practice than in theory.)

A second and particularly interesting example is the **Lord Chancellor** (**LC**). He used to combine not only two, but all three classes of function. As a Member of the Cabinet he was part of the executive, as **Speaker** of the House of Lords he played a legislative role, and he was the head of the English judiciary. However, this situation was also changed by the Constitutional Reform Act 2005. The House of Lords now elects a **Lord Speaker** to chair debates, and the head of the judiciary is now the Lord Chief Justice. The Lord Chancellor remains a member of Cabinet and is tasked with, for example, representing the interests of the judiciary and promoting diversity in judicial appointments. It is expected that the posts will usually be held by the Secretary of State for Justice (which is currently the case).

These recent changes have clearly strengthened the separation of powers, but some overlaps do remain, such as the fact that ministers are both members of the government and of Parliament, so they belong to both the executive and the legislature.

III. Parliament

1. Introduction

Parliament is the legislative body in the UK. It is organised as a **bi-cameral body**, consisting of two **Houses of Parliament**. The third part of Parliament is the Queen. The obvious function of the legislature is the making of laws. Parliament does this acting under the authority of the **Queen in Parliament**. However, this is not the only purpose of Parliament. It is also responsible for scrutinising national expenditure and provides a forum for the debate of matters of national interest. Both Houses meet in London in the **Palace of Westminster**.

2. The House of Commons

The **House of Commons** is the **Lower House** of Parliament. It is also often referred to simply as **'the Commons'** and consists of 646 **Members of Parliament** (**MPs**). The impartial chairman of the House is the **Speaker**; he or she calls Members to speak and ensures that order is maintained during debates.

Each MP represents a particular geographical district, called **constituency**, and the people living in it. MPs are elected at **general elections** which must take place at least every five years. If a **seat** in Parliament falls vacant between general elections, for example because an MP retires or dies, a **by-election** is held in the constituency in question.

Voting takes place using the **relative majority method**, also known as the **'first past the post'** system. The **candidate** who receives most votes in a constituency wins; there is no need for him to obtain a specific percentage of the votes cast. This means that if there are more than two candidates the winner may be supported by significantly less than half of the **electorate**. The main advantage of this **electoral system** is that there will usually be a strong one-party government; the principal disadvantage is that small parties tend to be under-represented.

The right to vote is governed by the general principle of **universal adult franchise**. A person will be allowed to vote provided that he is over 18 years old, resident in a parliamentary constituency and listed on the official **electoral register**. He must also show that he is not disqualified, for example because he is currently serving a prison sentence, has been found guilty of illegal election practices or is an **alien**. 'Alien' refers to persons who are not British citizens, but it does not include citizens of **Commonwealth** countries, who are entitled to vote.

Persons who wish to stand as candidates for election are subject to similar disqualifications as voters. The minimum age is 21 and certain people, such as aliens, bankrupts and convicted criminals serving a prison sentence cannot stand for election. The same applies to judges, civil servants, members of the police force and some others.

3. The House of Lords

The **House of Lords**, also referred to simply as **'the Lords'**, is the **Upper House** of Parliament. It currently has 724 members. It is a non-elected chamber, a peculiarity of the English system which has attracted an increasing amount of criticism over the years. This has led to plans for a full-scale reform of the chamber, a process which began in 1999, but is unlikely to be completed for some time yet.

The members of the Upper House, the **peers** and **peeresses**, can be divided into the **Lords Spiritual** and the **Lords Temporal**. The Lords Spiritual are members of the high clergy of the **Church of England**, such as the Archbishops of Canterbury and York, and the Bishops of Durham, London and Winchester. The Lords Temporal fall into two categories, namely **hereditary peers and life peers**. Life peers are appointed for life by the Queen on advice of the Prime Minister because of their service to the party or the public, and such **peerages** have been granted to politicians, **trade union** leaders, academics, industry leaders and doctors. They often introduce valuable expertise to the House of Lords, and have so far not been affected by the reform introduced in autumn 1999. A third category of Lords Temporal, the **Lords of Appeal in Ordinary**, lost their right to sit in the summer of 2009, when the House of Lords ceased to be the highest court in the country, and they became Justices of the new Supreme Court instead.

Hereditary peers are members of the nobility, such as dukes, earls and barons, who have inherited the right to sit in the House of Lords. Traditionally, this right was passed on from generation to generation. However, the **House of Lords Act 1999** abolished the right of hereditary peers to sit and vote in the House of Lords, thereby ending several hundred years of constitutional history. Only 92 of well over 700 hereditary peers (many of whom had never actually taken up their seat) were elected to remain members as an interim measure; their titles, like those of life peers, will cease on their death.

Currently many peers belong to one of the major political parties, and often vote in line with party policy (although they are not obliged to do so). There are also, however, a significant number of independent peers, commonly referred to as **cross-benchers.**

The exclusion of hereditary peers is only the first step in a planned total reform of the House of Lords. However, despite the publication of several Government **white papers,** there has been little progress. The House of Lords favours an appointed chamber, but the House of Commons has expressed strong support for a chamber that is 80 to 100 percent elected. Crossparty agreement has been reached on a number of issues (for example that members of the second chamber should have a single long term of office), but much remains to be decided. This includes how members should be elected and even the name of the new chamber. The current Government has stated that it expects the issue to be put to the electorate as a **manifesto** commitment by the leading parties. This suggests that there will be little progress until the next general election.

4. Government

The **government** is the executive branch of the State. Its work is divided into **government departments**, such as the **Home Office**, the **Department of Health**, the **Department for Children, Schools and Families** and the **Treasury**. The departments are staffed by **ministers of the Crown**, who are chosen by the **Prime Minister (PM)**, the leader of the government. Ministers who are in charge of a department are referred to as **secretary of state**, although some have special titles, such as the **Chancellor of the Exchequer**, who is the head of the Treasury. Other ranks of ministers include **ministers of state** and **junior ministers.**

The PM selects a group of senior ministers to form his **cabinet**. These **cabinet ministers** decide on government policy and co-ordinate the work of the individual departments. The cabinet will normally include the secretaries of state and the **Chief Whip. Whips** are appointed by each political party to facilitate communication between party leaders and members and to maintain discipline within the parliamentary party. They ensure, for example, that MPs attend important debates and votes.

The leader of the **opposition** will form his own **shadow cabinet** by appointing a counterpart for every member of the cabinet. In this way the opposition has a specialist available for every issue on which it may want to comment or challenge the government.

5. The Legislative Process

Both Houses participate in the legislative process. The general rule is that a measure must be **passed,** that is accepted, by both Houses and must receive **Royal Assent** before it becomes law.

Every Act of Parliament starts its life as a **bill,** the draft of a proposal for a new law. There are two kinds of bills, namely **public bills** and **private bills.** Public bills deal with matters of public policy which affect the public as a whole. Private bills are measures which affect only certain groups of persons, such as local authorities, universities and nationalised industries. The procedure for private bills is more complicated than that for public bills, to allow those affected to participate in the discussion.

Each public bill must be **sponsored** by a Member of Parliament. This means that he introduces the draft into Parliament. Bills which are sponsored by Ministers are called **Government bills**; those introduced by 'private', *i.e.* non-ministerial Members are **Private Member's bills** (not to be confused with private bills). Generally bills can be introduced in both Houses, but **money bills**, for example authorising taxation, must originate in the Commons. The procedure is the same for Government and Private Member's bills and involves three readings, a Committee stage and a Report stage.

The **first reading** is a mere formality. The title of the bill is read out and a date for the second reading is set. On **second reading** the general principles of the bill are debated by the House. The bill is then sent to a **Standing Committee**, or in some cases to a Committee of the whole House. In the Committee the individual clauses are discussed and **amendments**, *i.e.* changes to the provisions are suggested. The amended bill is then **reported** to the House. Members who were not on the Committee can also suggest amendments at this stage. The **third reading** is also often a formality only, any debate which does take place will normally be brief, and the bill is then presented to the House of Lords. The procedure in the Upper House is essentially the same as in the Commons, consisting of a formal first reading, debate in Committee and on Report and a third reading. However, there are no Standing Committees and the bill is always considered by the whole House. The bill is then sent back to the House of Commons together with any amendments suggested by the Lords. If these amendments are accepted by the Lower House the bill is presented for Royal Assent and becomes an Act of Parliament. If the House of Commons rejects the changes made by the House of Lords the bill can be sent for Royal Assent without the approval of the Lords one year later. The House of Lords can therefore only delay, but not defeat, a bill that has been accepted by the House of Commons. In the case of money bills the power of the Upper House is even more restricted, because they can only be delayed for a month. The final stage of the legislative process is Royal Assent. By convention the Queen does not refuse her Assent and the procedure is normally a formality only.

IV. Devolution

In 1998, Parliament adopted several pieces of legislation, which transferred some powers from central government in London to newly established bodies in Scotland, Wales and Northern Ireland. This decentralisation of governmental power is known as **devolution**.

In July 1999, the new **Scottish Parliament** met for the first time. It consists of 129 **Members of the Scottish Parliament** (**MSPs**), elected on the basis of a form of proportional representation called the **Additional Member System**. The **Scottish Government** consists of the **First Minister** and the **Cabinet Secretaries** and **ministers** appointed by him.

The Scottish Parliament has the power to adopt primary and secondary legislation on a large number of **devolved** matters, including agriculture, education, the environment, health, housing and local government. It also has some financial power, because it can vary the basic rate of income tax by a certain amount. However, other issues have been **reserved** for the **Westminster Parliament**. This means that all legislation on matters relating to the constitution, defence, employment, foreign affairs, social security and other reserved subjects will continue to be passed by Parliament in London, which remains the sovereign parliament of the UK.

Devolution to the newly formed **National Assembly for Wales**, which was also established in July 1999, has been less extensive. The Assembly has the power to develop and implement policies in areas such as agriculture, culture, education and training, housing and local government and it can decide how to allocate funds transferred to Wales by the Treasury. It can therefore pass secondary legislation, but cannot adopt its own primary legislation.

The Assembly consists of 60 **Members**, which are elected partly by the 'first past the post' system and partly by the Additional Member System, a form of proportional representation. The **Welsh Government** is lead by the **First Minister**, who forms a cabinet comprising **ministers** and **deputy ministers** of his choice.

The **Northern Ireland Assembly** was established in 1998 as an integral part of the peace process and the **Good Friday Agreement**. It has 108 **Members of the Legislative Assembly (MLAs)**, elected by proportional representation. The **Executive Committee** is headed by the **First Minister** and the **Deputy First Minister**. The Assembly has been given full legislative and executive authority in relation to a variety of matters, including education, the environment and health and social services.

The process of devolution of power to Northern Ireland has proved a difficult one, despite detailed rules as to power sharing between the **unionists** and the **nationalists**. After an initial breakdown in relations between the opposing parties, the Assembly met for the first time in November 1999. However, only eight weeks later it was suspended and power returned to the Government at Westminster, because of a lack of progress in the decommissioning of arms (a fundamental aim of the peace process). The Assembly was reinstated in May 2000 but suspended again in October 2002; power was finally restored to it in May 2007.

V. Terminology

Appointment of life peers: this demonstrates both a prerogative power and a constitutional convention in action. The appointment of life peers is a prerogative power of the Crown; the fact that it is only ever exercised in accordance with the advice of the Prime Minister is a convention.

Church of England: the established Protestant Church of England, also known as the **Anglican Church**. The sovereign is the supreme head, and must be a member.

Commonwealth: a voluntary organisation of independent states, including Britain and many former colonies. It is aimed at consultation and co-operation on a wide variety of matters. Key values include democracy, human rights and sustainable economic and social development. The Queen is recognised by all members as the symbol of their free association. The organisation is also known as the **British Commonwealth** or the **Commonwealth of Nations**.

Constitutional law: the term can refer to both the law actually contained in the constitution, and to the general area of law that deals with legal issues arising from the constitution.

Cross-benchers: the name derives from the fact that independent peers do not sit on either the side of the government or the opposition in the House of Lords, but on the benches that go across the floor at right angles to the opposing sides.

Dicey: Professor Albert Venn Dicey (1835 – 1922), jurist and legal writer. He is most famous for his 'Introduction to the Study of the Law of the Constitution'.

First past the post system: the rule that the winner does not need to have a certain percentage of the vote is strictly applied; he only needs to have one vote more than the second placed candidate.

Good Friday Agreement: an agreement signed in 1998, which sets out the future of Northern Ireland. It was negotiated by all the parties involved and was adopted by the people of Northern Ireland and Ireland in a referendum.

Government: spelt with a capital 'g' when a particular government, such as the present Government, is referred to. Government as a political institution is spelt without a capital.

Great Britain: constitutional law, unlike other law, applies to the whole of Great Britain.

Home Office: the Department responsible for all domestic matters which have not been assigned to a specialist Department; it therefore deals with issues such as the police and prisons, race relations and immigration.

Manifesto: a document setting out the strategic direction of a political party, as well as legislation it intends to introduce, should it win an election.

Money bill: a bill which concerns only certain financial matters, such as taxation, public money, or the raising of loans by the state.

Nationalists: those who are in favour of reuniting Ireland and Northern Ireland. They are mainly Catholics and are also referred to as **republicans**.

Opposition: generally all parties that are not the party in government are in opposition (so called because they sit opposite the government). The largest of these parties is known as **Her Majesty's Opposition**, headed by the **Leader of the Opposition**. It is this official opposition that will form a shadow cabinet.

Prime Minister: the actual title is **First Lord of the Treasury**.

Royal Assent: the formal expression of consent by the sovereign. The phrase used is Norman French: *la reyne le veult* (different phrases are used for private bills and monetary bills).

Standing Committee: a group of MPs convened in order to discuss the details of public bills at the relevant stage of the legislative process. They are set up to reflect the political composition of the House of Commons, and last only for the duration of the bill in question.

Trade union: an organisation of workers, whose aim it is to represent its members *vis-à-vis* their employers, and to protect their interests. Objects will usually include the raising of wages and the reduction of working hours; they can be obtained through negotiations or strikes.

Treasury: the Department responsible for finances and government spending.

Unionists: those who want Northern Ireland to remain part of the United Kingdom. They are mainly Protestants and are also referred to as **loyalists**.

Unwritten constitution: although Great Britain does have a constitution, it is not contained in a single written codified constitutional document.

Whip: the term refers to both the person who holds this office, and to the actual command issued to MPs, requiring them to be present at a certain vote. On the agenda of the week's business, the whips indicate the importance of every item by underlining it; a **'three-line whip'** (underlined three times) indicates that the party expects MPs to attend a vote (and to vote in line with the party). An MP's failure to obey a three-line whip is regarded as a serious matter.

White paper: a document issued by the government which sets out its policies on a particular issue and indicates a certain level of commitment to pass new legislation. It is often preceded by a **green paper**, a more open-ended document used to stimulate debate.

VI. Review and Discussion

1. *Explain the constitutional principle of Parliamentary sovereignty.*

One of the fundamental principles of British constitutional law is the concept of Parliamentary sovereignty. Parliament is the highest legislative authority in the country and can pass or repeal any piece of legislation it wishes. The courts can only intervene if a statute has not been passed according to the correct procedure; they cannot adjudicate on the contents of legislation. This is so even if an Act of Parliament were, for example, oppressive, discriminatory, or simply absurd. It should be kept in mind, however, that while there are no legal limits to what Parliament can do, there are nevertheless many practical considerations which restrict the absolute freedom of the legislator.

A second aspect of Parliamentary sovereignty is that there is no mechanism to safeguard a statute against being repealed. This is usually expressed as the maxim that Parliament cannot bind its successors.

2. *What is the relationship between the two Houses of Parliament?*

Parliament is divided into two bodies, the elected House of Commons and the non-elected House of Lords. Generally both must participate in order for legislation to be adopted. Thus bills can be introduced in either House, and must go through the same legislative process in each Chamber. However, the House of Commons is the more influential body. The most important factor is that the House of Lords can only delay, but not defeat a measure submitted to it by the Commons. A bill rejected by the Upper House does not become law immediately, but can receive Royal Assent a year later (a month later in the case of money bills), without the approval of the Lords being necessary.

3. *What is local government?*

Local government can briefly be described as the decentralisation of governmental power at regional level. **Local authorities** are bodies which are set up to deal with the administration of public affairs in a particular geographical area. They are subordinate to central government, but also have a considerable amount of discretionary powers in relation to the many different services they provide, which range from the building of roads to the provision of schools. In addition to these functions, local bodies can regulate certain activities in their area through by-laws. The members of local government are called **councillors**, and they are elected in regular **local elections**, which are organised in much the same way as general elections. **Councils** raise some money through the collection of

council tax (payable by people who live in the area), but most of their funds are allocated to them by the central government.

The system of local administration is quite complex, with five types of local authority in different parts of the country. A basic distinction can be drawn between **metropolitan** and **non-metropolitan** areas. Major conurbations, such as Manchester and Liverpool are administrated by **metropolitan district councils**. They are responsible for all services in their locality, with the exception of the fire and police services, which are run by separate bodies. In non-metropolitan areas there is a two-tier system of local government, consisting of **county councils** which are divided into several **district councils**. The larger county councils provide services such as education and social services, while the varied responsibility of district councils include housing, refuse collection, museums, parks and swimming pools. Some district councils have retained their traditional names of **borough** or **city council. Parish** or **town councils** are a third tier, but their powers are limited to matters like community halls and public clocks, and they do not exist everywhere. There are also some areas in which the functions of county and district councils have been merged into a single **unitary authority**.

London has its own system of local administration, the **Greater London Authority**, which consists of a directly elected **Mayor** and **Assembly**.

4. What do the Chambers of Parliament look like?

The Chamber of the House of Commons is a rectangular room, at one end of which stands the **Speaker's Chair. Benches** are arranged in tiers along two sides of the room, and government and opposition sit facing each other. In the middle in front of the Speaker's Chair stands the **Table of the House** with the **despatch box**, at which the Prime Minister stands to speak. Ministers sit in the front row, closest to the Speaker's Chair, as do opposition spokesmen on the other side. They are therefore often referred to as **frontbenchers**, while all other MP's are **backbenchers**. It is interesting to note that the Chamber only provides room for 437 MP's to sit, even though there are 646 members in total.

The Chamber of the House of Lords has seats on three sides of the room, the fourth being occupied by the Throne. As in the Lower House, government and opposition sit facing each other, while independent peers sit on the rows that are effectively in between. The Speaker sits on a large square cushion called the **Woolsack**, which is filled with wool from all over the Commonwealth.

There are two noticeable differences between the two Chambers. The House of Commons is upholstered in green, while the House of Lords is red. Furthermore, the Upper House is elaborately decorated, while the Lower House is much less ornate, almost austere in comparison.

Chapter 9: Equity and Trusts

I. Historical Development of Equity

It is almost impossible to give a simple short definition of equity. The concept is best understood in the light of its historical development.

1. Development of the Court of Chancery

In order to start an action in the common law courts the claimant (at that time called **plaintiff**) needed to obtain a **writ.** However, only a limited number of causes of action were recognised, and if the claimant's case did not fall within an established writ, the common law courts did not provide a remedy. Even a claimant who had cleared this first hurdle might find himself prevented from obtaining or enforcing a judgment in his favour, by the wealth and influence of the defendant.

Often the only recourse for claimants who had failed to obtain justice from the common law courts was to **petition** the King, asking him to exercise his discretionary power to provide a remedy. Although these petitions were addressed to the King and Council they were in fact usually dealt with by the **Chancellor.** As the rigidity of the common law increased and more and more claimants were left without a remedy for their grievances, petitions to the King multiplied, and after some time they were addressed directly to the Chancellor rather than the King.

Most of the early Chancellors were bishops and their ecclesiastical background was reflected in the way they dealt with the petitions that came before them. Decisions were based on their individual sense of right and wrong and were strongly influenced by ideas such as fairness and morality. Later the Chancellors were often lawyers, and consequently they adopted a more legalistic approach. The way in which petitions were dealt with became increasingly systematic; precise rules and principles were developed, which made decisions more predictable. Gradually the Chancellor's Department, the **Chancery**, began to operate like a court and became known as the **Court of Chancery**. The rules and principles that were applied by the Court of Chancery became known as **equity**.

In addition to the fact that no writ was necessary in order to petition the Chancellor, the Court of Chancery offered the claimant a number of important procedural advantages which were not available in the common law courts. The defendant could be compelled to appear before the Court to answer the claim by the threat of the forfeiture of a sum of money, a so-called **subpoena**. In addition he had to give evidence under oath. There was no jury, so the defendant could not escape judgment by bribing or threatening the jurors. Likewise he could not use his wealth or influence to prevent the enforcement of the judgment, because the decisions of the Chancellor could be enforced by threats of imprisonment. In order to ensure that his judgment was not simply ignored the Chancellor could issue injunctions which prevented the defendant from taking the matter in question to a common law court or from enforcing a common law judgment in his favour. These injunctions were also backed by the threat of imprisonment.

By issuing such injunctions equity was clearly interfering with the jurisdiction of the common law courts and this led to a period of clashes between the common law courts and the Court of Chancery. The conflict was resolved by James I, who decided that the Court of Chancery could continue to issue injunctions.

2. The Fusion of Law and Equity

During the nineteenth century a piecemeal reform of equity took place, which was aimed, amongst other things, at dealing with the enormous increase in the case load of the Court of Chancery. The reforms culminated in the **Judicature Acts 1873-75**, which established a unified court system to apply both common law and equity. The old common law courts were abolished and their jurisdiction transferred to the individual divisions of the new High Court. Today each division has **complete jurisdiction**, *i.e.* it can deal with both equity and law. The Judicature Acts 1873-75 thus effected the **fusion** of law and equity, or rather the fusion of the administration of law and equity, as the distinction between equitable and legal rights and remedies continues to exist. It was laid down in the Judicature Acts that, should a conflict arise between the two, equity will prevail.

II. Maxims of Equity

1. Nature of Equitable Maxims

Equitable maxims contain the fundamental principles of equity; they are illustrations of the essential concepts which underlie equitable jurisdiction. Although the way in which they are phrased can make them seem like binding rules, they are in fact guidelines only; nevertheless one should always be aware of them when considering equitable doctrines.

2. Examples of Equitable Maxims

It is not possible in this context to provide a complete list of the twelve equitable maxims, therefore only a few examples will be given.

He who seeks equity must do equity. A person will only be granted an equitable remedy if he is himself prepared to act fairly towards the other party; for example, rescission of a contract will only be granted if the claimant is willing and able to return all benefits he received under that contract to the defendant.

He who comes to equity must come with clean hands. The claimant must not be guilty of unconscionable conduct. This principle is closely related to the first one; the difference between the two is that the former refers to the claimant's future conduct, while the latter takes his previous conduct into account. Operating together these maxims allow the court to evaluate not only the behaviour of the defendant, but also that of the claimant.

Delay defeats equity. The courts will not grant an equitable remedy to someone who has failed to assert his rights within a reasonable time and has thereby created the impression that these rights have been waived. This principle is also known as the doctrine of **laches**.

Equity acts *in personam*. The jurisdiction of equity attaches to the defendant personally. This means that the courts can deal with a dispute, even if the subject-matter is outside their territorial jurisdiction, provided that the defendant himself is within the jurisdiction of the courts.

Equity looks to the intent rather than the form. Equity will look at the substance rather than the form of a transaction or arrangement to determine the intention of the parties. Thus if property is transferred from one party to the other by way of security, equity will regard this as a mortgage, even if the word 'mortgage' was not actually used by the parties. However, this does not mean that all formalities can be ignored in equity.

III. Equitable Remedies

1. Introduction

The range of available remedies at common law is very limited. The main remedy is an award of damages, but money cannot always adequately compensate the claimant for the loss he has suffered. Equity therefore developed a number of **equitable remedies** to provide relief in those situations where damages are inadequate. Equitable remedies are available to enforce both legal and equitable rights and are of great practical importance.

All equitable remedies share a number of important characteristics that distinguish them from **legal remedies**. First, equitable remedies are always **discretionary**. This means that in every case the court has a choice whether or not to grant the relief sought. In exercising its discretion the court may, for example, look at the conduct of the claimant according to the **'clean hands'** principle discussed above. Damages, on the other hand, are available **as of right**, *i.e.* they must be awarded if the claimant has established his entitlement; the court cannot take any other considerations, such as fairness, into account.

Secondly, equitable remedies will only be granted if the legal remedies are inadequate. A claimant who can be fully compensated for his loss by an award of damages will not obtain an equitable remedy.

Finally, the principle that equity acts *in personam* also applies to equitable remedies. They will not be granted if they cannot be enforced against the defendant personally.

The main equitable remedies are specific performance, injunctions, rescission and rectification.

2. Specific Performance

Specific performance is a remedy which is granted in cases of breach of contract. The party in breach is ordered to perform, *i.e.* to fulfil his obligations under the contract. There are certain types of contracts where specific performance is almost always awarded, such as contracts for the sale of land; as each piece of land is unique damages will normally be inadequate to compensate the claimant. Contracts of employment, on the other hand, are never specifically enforced, as it is laid down by statute that a court cannot force an employee to work.

3. Injunctions

An **injunction** is an order of the court directing a person to do or refrain from doing a specified act. Injunctions are a very important remedy, especially in relation to areas like trespass and nuisance. There are different categories of injunctions, relating to their content, their finality or the way in which they are issued.

a) Prohibitory and Mandatory Injunctions

The **prohibitory injunction** is the most common type of injunction. It is restrictive, it restrains the doing or continuance of an act. For example, a court may issue such an injunction to stop a person from building a wall that intrudes on neighbouring property. If the wrongful act has already been committed, the defendant may be ordered to undo what he has done. Such an order is called a **mandatory injunction**. In the example given above the defendant would be ordered to pull down the wall which he has built on neighbouring property.

b) Final and Interim Injunctions

A **final injunction** (also called **perpetual injunction**) is only granted after a case has been heard by the court in the normal way and the claimant has proved that his rights are being infringed by the defendant. The order is the final conclusion of the dispute between the parties. However, it can take some time before a case is brought to trial, and in certain circumstances the claimant may already have suffered irreparable damage when the case is finally heard. In these situation the claimant can apply for an **interim injunction.** Such an injunction does not require a full hearing of the case; it is sufficient if the claimant shows that the dispute is sufficiently serious to require consideration by the court. The order is effective until the case is brought before court in the normal course of proceedings.

c) Without Notice Injunctions

Normally an application for an injunction must be made **on notice**, that is in the presence of both parties. However, in very urgent cases the claimant may not be able to wait until notice of the application has been served on the defendant. The application can then be made **without notice**, *i.e.* in the absence of the other party. The injunction will be valid until the defendant has been notified of the application and an on notice hearing will then take place. The claimant must show a strong case before a court will grant an injunction without hearing the opinion of the defendant.

d) Freezing Injunctions and Search Orders

Both orders are relatively recent developments and illustrate the fact that equity is not stationary, but continues to develop. The **freezing injunction** prevents the defendant from removing his assets from, or dissipating them within, the jurisdiction. It is aimed at avoiding a situation in which the claimant has obtained a judgment in his favour, but cannot enforce it, because the defendant has taken all his money out of the reach of the court. A **search order** instructs the defendant to allow the claimant entry onto his premises for the purpose of inspecting specified documents. It is granted in situations in which the claimant needs documents that are in the possession of the defendant as evidence to support his claim.

4. Rescission

The right to **rescind** a contract is the right of one party to set the contract aside and to be restored to his former position. **Rescission** exists both at common law and in equity, but in equity the concept is much wider than at law, for example in relation to the circumstances in which the right to rescind arises. The aim of rescission is ***restitutio in integrum***, *i.e.* the claimant should, as far as possible, be restored to the position he would be in if the contract had never been entered into.

5. Rectification

When the parties to a contract set down their agreement in an instrument it may happen that they make a mistake so that the document does not in fact accurately reflect their intentions. In such a situation the court can order **rectification.** This means that the mistakes in the instrument are corrected so that it accords with the intention of the parties. It should be noted that the court will only **rectify** a mistake in the document which records the contract; it will not correct a mistake in the contract itself.

IV. Trusts

1. Historical Development of the Trust

The forerunner of the modern trust was the medieval **use**, where land was owned by one person **'to the use'**, *i.e.* **for the benefit** of another. There were various reasons why this might be done. If A, the owner of a particular piece of land, went on crusade he needed someone to perform and receive feudal services; he would therefore convey the land to X, to hold for the benefit, 'to the use' of himself, A, until his return. A might also want to ensure that his family was cared for while he was away, and he could do this by transferring the land to X to the use of B, A's wife. Finally, A might employ the use to avoid having to pay the feudal lord a certain sum of money when his heir succeeded to the land. If the land was held by X to the use of A, and A's son C succeeded A as the person who benefited from the use, the feudal lord did not receive any money, because the land was and remained the legal property of X.

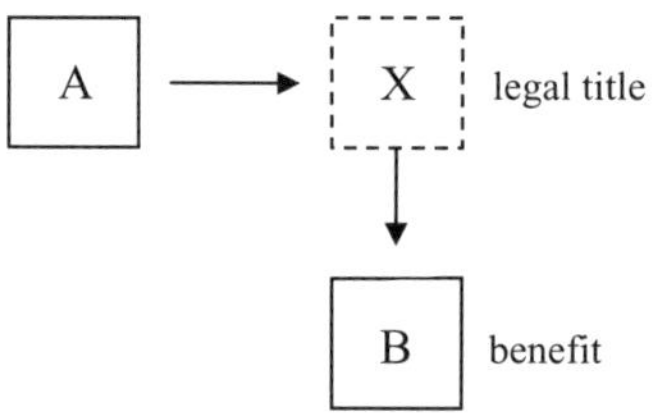

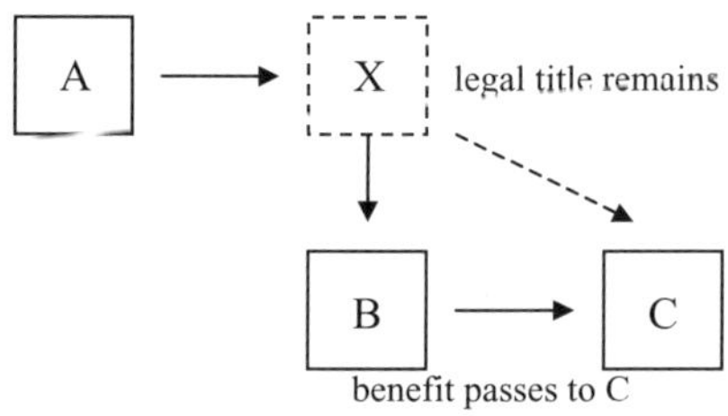

The rights of the person who was supposed to benefit from the use were not recognised and therefore not protected by the common law. X was the **legal owner** of the land and could do with it whatever he wished; at common law, B could not sue to enforce the terms of the use (obviously A could sue X, but this was often of no practical significance, as A would usually be away on crusade or dead). The Chancellor, on the other hand, began to recognise the rights of people like B and C. Equity regarded X as bound by his conscience to fulfil the intention of the use, and declared the persons who were intended to benefit from the land to be the **equitable owners.**

As the practice of employing uses to avoid feudal payments increased, the King (the highest feudal lord) began losing significant parts of his income. He tried to restrict the creation of uses in the **Statute of Uses** of 1535. It provided that where a use was created it should be **executed** so that the person who was supposed to benefit from the land (A, B or C) became the **full legal owner.** However, in time people found a way of operating around the Statute of Uses by simply imposing a second use on top of the first one. Land was transferred from A (the original owner) to Y to the use of X to the use of B; under the Statute the first use (Y to the use of X) was executed and X became the full legal owner. However, because of the second use (X to the use of B), which was not covered by the statute, X held the land not for himself, but for the benefit of B. This second use was called a **trust**. In time Y was omitted completely and the land was transferred from A 'unto and to the use of X in trust for B'.

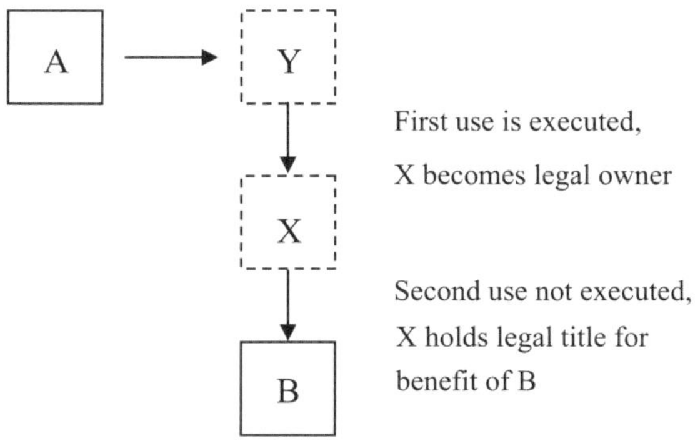

2. Definition of the Trust

It is very difficult to give a simple definition of the **trust**. Most definitions are either short, but fail to cover all the different types of trusts, or they are complete, but so long that they are descriptions rather than definitions.

A trust is a particular legal relationship whereby property is transferred from one person to another, who controls it for the benefit of a third person, or for a specified purpose. Although the assets in question are vested **in the name** of one person, they are not part of his own estate. He is not free to apply them according to his own wishes; he must observe the terms of the trust and comply with special duties imposed on him by law. The property which is subject to the trust is called the **trust fund**. It can consist of all kinds of property, such as money in a bank account, land and shares in a company.

3. The Private Express Trust

The **private express trust** is the paradigm of the trust. It is created by an express declaration, which means that, unlike some other forms of trust, it corresponds with the intention of the person who set it up. This declaration can be very informal and need not even contain the word 'trust'.

The person who creates the trust is the **settlor**. He transfers the property to a person of his choice, who becomes the **trustee**. The trustee has the **legal title** to the property, so that **in law** he is the full owner. However, the trustee is required to **hold** the property **on trust** for yet another person, namely the **beneficiary**. It is the beneficiary and not the trustee who has the actual benefit of the property in question; he has the **beneficial** or **equitable title** to the property – **in equity** he is the owner.

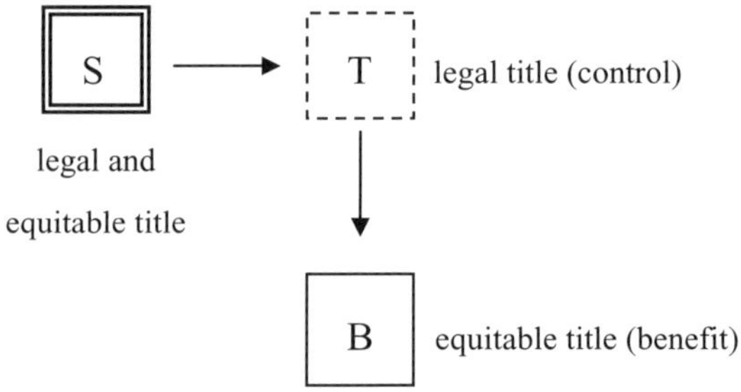

The following example will illustrate the private express trust. The settlor wishes to provide for the future education of his granddaughter, who is still a minor. He owns a house that is rented to a third party, and wishes to use the income from the lease to pay for her education. He transfers the legal title in the house to his son as trustee, instructing him to hold it on trust for the granddaughter, the beneficiary. The trustee is then obliged to collect the rent paid by the tenant of the house and to use it to pay for the education of his daughter.

4. Purpose Trusts

Some trusts are set up not for the benefit of a particular person or group of persons, but rather for a particular purpose. These so-called **purpose trusts** are usually invalid, precisely because no beneficiaries are identified. An exception is made for purpose trusts that are classified as charitable.

5. Charitable Trusts

Purpose trusts will be valid if they qualify as **charitable trusts** as defined by the **Charities Act 2006**. They must be for a recognised charitable purpose and for public benefit. A non-exhaustive list of such purposes is given in the statute and includes the advancement of education, environmental protection, amateur sports and arts, and the prevention or relief of poverty. Charitable trusts are granted certain significant advantages, such as tax benefits.

6. Constructive and Resulting Trusts

Unlike, for example, a private express trust, a **constructive trust** arises by operation of law and not as a result of the intention of a settlor. Constructive trusts are imposed in a variety of situations. For instance such a trust will be imposed if a trustee makes an unauthorised profit from the trust fund. He will not be allowed to keep the money, instead he will hold it on constructive trust for the beneficiaries.

Under a **resulting trust** the trustee is obliged to hold the property on trust for the settlor. If the settlor tries to set up an express trust and transfers the property to the trustee, but fails to name the beneficiaries, the trust is void and the benefit **reverts back** to the settlor under an **automatic resulting trust**, meaning that the trustee holds the assets in trust for the settlor.

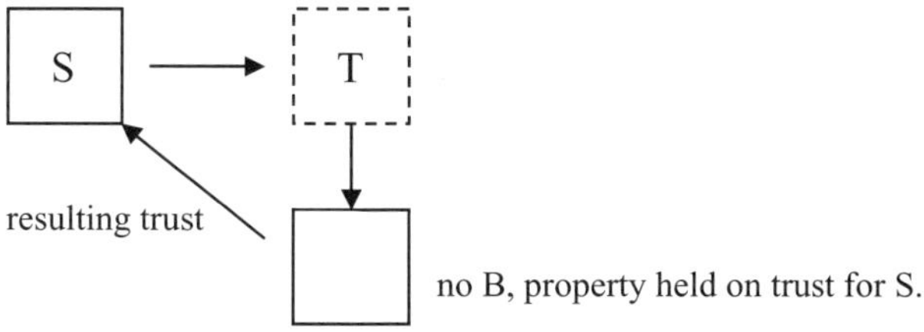

In certain other circumstances the law presumes an intention to create a trust (even though there is no clear evidence), for example where a wife has contributed to the purchase price of a house that is registered in her husband's name only. This is known as a **presumed resulting trust.**

7. Fiduciary Duties

The trustee has a large number of duties in relation to the trust, because he is in a **fiduciary relationship** with the beneficiary. A **fiduciary** is a person who may not use his position to gain a benefit for himself; it is expected that he will act in the best interest of another, in this case the beneficiary, rather than in his own interest. The trustee must diligently carry out all obligations imposed by the trust. If he is given a choice, for example concerning the investment of the trust fund, he must act in the way which is in the best interest of the beneficiary. He must not place himself in a position in which there is a conflict between his own interest and those of the beneficiary.

8. Tracing

The process of **tracing** allows the beneficiary to follow up and recover assets which a **defaulting trustee** has appropriated from the trust fund. To a limited extent tracing is possible at common law, but it is much more developed in equity.

The following example will illustrate the process of tracing. The trust fund in question is money in a bank account. The trustee withdraws money from this account without being authorised to do so. He uses the money to buy shares in a company, again without authorisation. Later he sells those shares with profit and buys a house and a car. The beneficiary can trace the appropriated money through all the changes in its nature and can claim title to the house and the car.

V. Terminology

Beneficiary: also called ***cestui que trust*** (plural: ***cestuis que trust***).

Chancellor: the highest ranking ministerial officer, keeper of the king's seal and chaplain to the king. He came to be regarded as the second most important person in the country, and acted as representative of the king.

Constructive and resulting trust: some confusion has been caused by the fact that these terms are not always clearly distinguished, and have at times been used interchangeably.

Defaulting trustee: a trustee is **in default** if he has in some way breached his fiduciary duties, for example by taking money from the trust fund for his own purposes.

Fiduciary: is used both as a noun (as in 'a trustee is a fiduciary') and an adjective (as in 'a trustee owes fiduciary duties'). Other examples of fiduciary relationships include solicitor and client and agent and principal.

Full legal owner: has both the legal and the beneficial title to property. A trustee is not a full legal owner, as only the legal, but not the equitable, title is vested in him; he has a **bare legal title**.

Plaintiff: the person bringing a case used to be called the plaintiff, but is now called the claimant (terminology changed by the Civil Procedure Rules 1998). It should be kept in mind that pre-1999 books will use the old term plaintiff.

Subpoena: literally 'under a penalty'. Subpoenas are still used today to ensure that witnesses appear in court.

Writ: writs were framed at quite an early stage in the development of English law. Therefore they covered only the most common and obvious causes of action. Changes in society lead to the recognition of new legal rights and duties, for example in relation to property, for which the existing writs did not provide a remedy. The ensuing rigidity of the common law, together with various procedural shortcomings, lead to the increase of petitions to the King, and, ultimately, to the development of equity. Writs are still needed to begin a court case, but are now called claim forms.

VI. Review and Discussion

1. *What is the relationship between common law and equity?*

Initially equity developed to fill the gaps left by an overly rigid common law. The two systems remained separate for a long time, each with its own principles, remedies and courts. The Judicature Acts 1873-75 created a new system of courts, with jurisdiction to apply both law and equity. Where there is a direct conflict between the two systems, equity prevails over the common law. While the Judicature Acts clearly fused the administration of law and equity, they did not completely combine the systems themselves. Clear distinctions remain between legal rights and remedies on the one hand and equitable rights and remedies on the other.

2. *What is a trust?*

Property rights can be both legal and equitable in nature. A person who has complete ownership of, for example, a piece of land, has both the legal and the equitable title. If the land is subject to a trust, however, the two elements of ownership are vested in different people. The trustee is the legal owner, but he cannot use the property for his own benefit. He must always act in the best interest of the beneficiary, who holds the equitable title. The trust fund is not part of the general assets of the trustee; thus it does not pass to his heirs in the event of the trustee's death. Trusts can arise by express declaration or by operation of law.

3. *What is equitable estoppel?*

There are several types of equitable estoppel. **Promissory estoppel**, for example, arises where one person (X) makes a promise to another (Y) regarding his future conduct, which affects their legal relationship. If Y changes his position in reliance on that promise, X cannot later change his mind, if to do so would be unfair towards Y; he is **estopped** from acting in a way which is inconsistent with his earlier representation.

Promissory estoppel is an exception to the general rule that a promise must be supported by consideration to be binding; thus if X assures Y that it is sufficient if he pays half of the money he owes X, this promise will be enforced (even in the absence of consideration), if it would be inequitable to allow X to claim the remainder of the money.

In cases of **proprietary estoppel** X has led Y to believe that he (Y) has (or will acquire) some rights in relation to property belonging to X. If this promise induces Y to act to his detriment, X will be held bound by his representation. Thus, if Y believed that she was acquiring a share of the matrimonial home (legal title to which is vested in her husband X only) by making contributions to the mortgage repayments, X is estopped from denying that she has in fact acquired such a share.

Promissory and proprietary estoppel are closely related, but there are important differences between them. One of these is that only proprietary estoppel gives rise to an independent cause of action, *i.e.* it is possible to bring a claim against someone else on this basis. Promissory estoppel can only be used as a defence, *i.e.* when one is being sued.

4. *What are the three certainties?*

A private express trust will only be valid if it meets all **three certainties. Certainty of intention** requires that the settlor's intention to create a trust is made clear. The word 'trust' does not have to be used, and indeed intention can be inferred from the settlor's conduct, but the aim of splitting legal and equitable ownership must be evident, otherwise there will be no valid trust. The second part of the certainty requirement is **certainty of subject-matter** – the clear identification of the property which is to constitute the trust fund. The definition of the relevant assets must be objective, rather than subjective, so that there can be no difference of opinion as to what should be the subject-matter of the trust. Thus a phrase like 'a significant part of my money' would not be sufficiently certain, because people can disagree as to what would be 'a significant part'. A trust cannot be complete without someone to take the benefit, and therefore the intended beneficiaries must also be identified with sufficient precision. This is referred to as **certainty of objects**. The beneficiaries do not need to be named, it is sufficient if a list of objects is ascertainable. In the absence of clearly identified or identifiable beneficiaries, the trustee will hold the property for the settlor under a resulting trust.

Chapter 10: Contract Law

I. Introduction

A **contract** is a voluntary agreement between two or more parties, which creates **legally enforceable obligations**. There are various forms of legal obligations, which arise, for example, from the law of torts or restitution. The distinguishing feature of contractual obligations is that they are based on the agreement of the parties concerned, whereas other legal obligations can arise, not only without the agreement of the parties, but even against their wishes. It should be noted, however, that this is a basic and imprecise distinction, as even contracts are not always based on agreement.

The law of contract deals mainly with four issues. Firstly, is there an agreement at all? Secondly, if there is an agreement should it be legally enforced? Thirdly, what are its contents? And fourthly, how can it be enforced?

A contract which creates binding obligations will be enforced by the courts. Mere social arrangements such as an informal invitation to dinner are not binding and therefore cannot be legally enforced. Although the difference between a binding contract and social arrangement is normally obvious it can at times be difficult to decide to which category a particular arrangement belongs.

II. Formation of a Contract

1. Freedom of Contract

The principle of **freedom of contract** consists of two elements, namely the freedom to decide whether or not to enter into a contract and the freedom to decide on what terms to contract. Generally it can be said that everybody can refuse to enter into a particular type of contract, or into a contract with a particular person, whatever the reason for his decision might be. When a contract is formed the parties alone determine the contents of their agreement; the courts will not interfere simply because one party is in a stronger bargaining position and the terms are unfair towards the other.

When the concept of freedom of contract was developed in the nineteenth century it accorded with the general philosophy of *laissez-faire* which prevailed at the time. Since then, however, the law has recognised that true freedom of contract does not always exist. A consumer who is presented with the standard form contract of a monopoly supplier in practice has very little influence on the terms of the contract. The principle of freedom of contract has therefore been restricted in areas such as consumer sales to avoid abuse and protect those who are generally regarded as the weaker parties to a contract.

The freedom to decide whether or not to enter into a contract at all has likewise been restricted on grounds of public policy, so that in certain situations a person can no longer refuse to enter into a contract because of the sex or race of another.

2. Offer and Acceptance

As was stated above, a contract is an agreement between two parties. This agreement comes into existence when one party makes an offer which is accepted by the other party.

An **offer** is a statement to the effect that the person making it is willing to enter into a contract, provided that the party to whom it is addressed accepts the terms of the offer.

This statement must be made with the intention that it shall be binding as soon as the offer has been accepted. The person making the offer is called **offeror**, the person to whom the offer is made is the **offeree**. Once the offeree has received the offer he can either agree or decline to enter into a contract with the offeror. If he decides to accept the offer, he must do so without changing the terms in any way; the **acceptance** will only be valid if it is an unqualified and final expression of assent to the terms of the offer. As soon as acceptance of the offer has been communicated by the offeree to the offeror, a binding contract is concluded between them.

3. Consideration

A **bilateral contract** consists of two promises. If A and B form a contract that B will buy A's car, both parties promise that they will carry out the contract and will sell, respectively buy, the car. In English law a promise is only binding if it is supported by **consideration.** Under this doctrine, which is unique to the common law, every contract must contain an element of **reciprocity**. The contract is viewed as a **bargain** and each party must give something in return for what he receives from the other. In most contracts, such as the example given above, consideration is obvious; A receives the money from B, B receives the car. If, however, A promises a **gratuitous gift** to B, *i.e.* to give him the car as a present, and then changes his mind B cannot enforce the promise because he has not provided any consideration.

A contract can also consist of a promise by one party and the performance of an act by the other. This is called a **unilateral contract**, and the most common example is the situation where A offers a reward of £100 to the person who returns his lost dog. The central feature of this arrangement is that A is bound by his promise; if B finds the dog, A must pay him £100. B, on the other hand, is not obliged to do anything; he does not have to go looking for the dog and he can even start searching and then stop. Just like a bilateral contract, a unilateral contract must be supported by consideration to be binding. A's consideration is his promise to pay £100, while B provides consideration by performing the requested act. Returning the dog thus constitutes both consideration for A's promise to pay, and performance of the contract.

The courts have developed a number of specific rules of consideration relating to, for example, who consideration must be provided by and whom it must be provided to. It is more difficult to determine what consideration can or must consist of. It has long been accepted that in order to constitute **valid** consideration whatever is given in return for the promise of the other party must be of 'some value in the eyes of the law'. Unfortunately it is not possible to give a detailed list of things which are of 'some value'; consideration can consist of a large number of different things, depending on the kind of contract in question. Generally it can be said that whatever is given in return must be either a **benefit** to the **promisor** or a **detriment** to the **promisee**.

The function of the doctrine of consideration is to distinguish between binding and non-binding agreements. The courts will not use consideration to judge the fairness of a bargain. Consideration must be **sufficient**, but need not be **adequate**. This means that consideration must be of some value (sufficient), but it need not be of the same economic value as that which it is given in return for (adequate). Therefore consideration can be valid even though it is **nominal**. Nominal consideration is also called **'peppercorn'** consideration, because a promise to give, for example, a car in return for a peppercorn, *i.e.* something with very small economic value, is binding.

Consideration can consist of an act or forbearance or the promise of either. It is said to be **executory** if one party gives a promise in return for the promise or act of the other. That means, where both parties agree to do something in the future each promise is consideration for the other. Where one party performs an act in return for a promise or act the consideration is **executed.**

4. Form

A contract is said to require a certain **form** if it has to be recorded in a specific way laid down by law. The general rule of English law is that contracts can be entered into without the parties having to adhere to a particular form. However, there are exceptions to this rule. Contracts for the sale of land, for example, have to be in **writing.** This means that the terms of the contract must be set out or at least referred to in one document. The second common formal requirement is the **deed.** A deed is a written instrument which must be signed by the person making it and must be witnessed by at least one witness. In addition it must be clear from the face of the document that it is intended to be a deed.

A contract which is not in the prescribed form is not legally enforceable; form is therefore a necessary requirement of enforceability. In the case of a deed, however, form is also a sufficient requirement, as a contract that is made in a deed need not be supported by consideration. Thus even a gratuitous promise can be binding if it is made in a deed.

5. Intention to Create Legal Relations

Agreement and consideration are the first two requirements of a binding contract. The third is an **intention to create legal relations.** This exists if the parties intend that any dispute which might arise from the contract will be resolved by a court.

Where the agreement is between businessmen, *i.e.* a commercial transaction, the question of contractual intention will not normally be raised. The court will presume that such an intention existed, unless one party can positively prove that this was not the case, for example because the parties had expressly provided for a 'gentlemen's agreement'. Exactly the opposite presumption is commonly applied to family arrangements; here the court will assume that the agreement was not intended to be legally binding. It is of course open to the parties to show that in their case the necessary intention did exist.

III. Contents of the Contract

1. Express and Implied Terms

A contract is often the result of prolonged negotiations between the parties and not everything that was said during those discussions will eventually become part of the agreement. Those statements of the parties which do become binding terms of the contract are called **express terms.** They have to be distinguished from mere **representations,** comments made prior to the formation of the contract which were made in order to induce the other party to enter into the contract, but which are not part of the contract itself.

In addition to express terms a contract may also contain **implied terms,** *i.e.* terms which were not expressly agreed on by the parties. There are three types of implied terms.

Terms implied in fact. A term implied in fact is one which, in the opinion of the court, the parties must have intended to include in the contract, even though they did not expressly include it. Such a term will only be implied if it is 'so obvious that it goes without saying', for example something without which the contract cannot work.

Terms implied in law. When terms are implied in law they are not based on the presumed intention of the parties; they are based on policy and are imported into a contract by operation of law. Many of these terms have been developed in relation to particular contracts, such as contracts of employment, and are now set out in the relevant statutes. They are often designed to protect one of the parties, and cannot be excluded, regardless of what the contract says.

Terms implied by custom. The parties to a contract will be expected to take account of all trade usages and customs that exist in the relevant commercial field. They will even be bound by a custom of which they were unaware, provided that it is not inconsistent with the express or implied terms of the contract.

2. Conditions, Warranties and Innominate Terms

Not all terms of a contract carry equal weight. Traditionally the law recognised two classes of contractual terms, namely conditions and warranties; a third one has now been added in the form of innominate terms. The importance of the distinction lies in the different remedies that are available when a contractual term is breached.

A **condition** is a term which is so important that in the case of breach the innocent party is entitled to claim damages and **terminate** the contract, if he so wishes. Breach of a **warranty**, on the other hand, only leads to the right to claim damages; the victim cannot terminate the contract. By way of simplification it can be said that conditions are the main terms of the contract, while warranties deal with the more subsidiary issues. **Innominate terms** are an intermediate category between conditions and warranties. They are therefore also called **intermediate terms**. The remedy that is available for breach of such a term depends on the severity of the breach in the individual case. The injured party can always claim damages, but the right to terminate the contract only exists if the breach amounts to a serious failure of performance.

3. Standard Form Contracts

Standard form contracts are very common today. They are drawn up in advance by one party and presented to all potential contracting partners. There are no individual negotiations between the parties and the person who is presented with the contract normally only has the choice of accepting or rejecting it; he cannot influence the terms.

While standard form contracts offer many advantages to the parties who use them, because they save time and effort, they are also open to abuse. They are often used *vis-à-vis* consumers who are not in the position to resist the imposition of unfair terms, even if they read the proverbial 'small print'. **Exemption clauses** cause particular problems in this respect. Such clauses, also called **exclusion clauses**, exclude or limit the liability of one party to a contract for conduct on his part which amounts to negligence or breach of contract. In order to avoid misuse of such clauses special statutory rules now apply to exemption clauses.

IV. Contracts and Third Parties

1. Privity of Contract and the Contract (Rights of Third Parties) Act 1999

Under the rule of **privity of contract** a contract can confer rights and impose obligations only on the parties to it. Someone who is not a party to a contract cannot generally sue or be sued under it, *i.e.* he cannot enforce rights created by the contract and obligations arising under it cannot be enforced against him.

This rule is unproblematic as far as the imposition of duties is concerned, because it should not be possible for the contracting parties simply to impose obligations on someone else without his agreement, but it is not so easy to justify why a contract cannot confer a benefit on a third party. There are many situations where the parties may wish to do so, and the need to give effect to their intentions led to the development of various exceptions, including the **Contract (Rights of Third Parties) Act 1999**. This provides that a **third party** (someone who is not a party to the agreement) can nevertheless enforce rights under that contract, provided that this was the intention of the contracting parties and that certain conditions are met.

2. Agency

Agency is a relationship under which one person, the **agent**, is authorised to act as a representative of another, the **principal**. If the agent enters into a contract with a third party he does so on behalf of the principal and it is the principal, not the agent who is bound by the agreement. This contract between principal and third party must be distinguished from the contract between principal and agent, which is the basis of the relationship of agency between them.

V. Void and Voidable Contracts

1. Meaning of 'Void' and 'Voidable'

A contract may either be valid or invalid to a greater or lesser degree by being void, voidable or unenforceable.

'Void' means that an agreement which was intended to be binding, is in fact not a contract at all and does not produce any legal effects. If one party fails to perform the other cannot sue for breach of contract. This will be the case if, for example, the parties agreed on the sale of goods which, unknown to them, were destroyed before the contract was made. Benefits which have been transferred, for example if one party has already paid, must be returned, as the agreement is void ***ab initio*** (from the beginning), meaning that it is treated as though it had never existed.

In some situations it is up to one of the parties to decide whether or not the legal relations created by the contract should continue to exist; he has a right of **election**. This right to **rescind** the contract is granted in a variety of situations, such as misrepresentation, and the contract is said to be **voidable**. The party entitled to chose can either **affirm** the contract or **avoid** it. **Affirmation** extinguishes the right of **avoidance** and the contract has the full legal effect it was intended to produce. If the contract is avoided, both parties are again returned to their original position.

A contract that is neither void nor voidable may nevertheless be **unenforceable**. This is the case if one or both parties cannot be sued under the contract, even though the contract itself is valid. A contract is unenforceable if, for example, the limitation period for its enforcement has expired.

2. Capacity

Capacity refers to a person's ability to enter into a binding contract. The general rule of English law is that anyone can do so. However, there are some important exceptions to this rule, for example in relation to **minors**, mentally ill persons and intoxicated persons, who all lack contractual capacity.

Young children, patients suffering from mental disorders and people who are drunk cannot form the necessary intention to create a binding contract, but older teenagers will usually be capable of doing so. Nevertheless they cannot normally enter into binding contracts, because it is the policy of the law that they should be protected from their own inexperience.

3. Illegality

Under the principle of freedom of contract there are no restrictions on what the parties to a contract can agree on. However, there are exceptions to this principle, for example the rules on **illegality**. The law does not enforce contracts which are in some way illegal.

Broadly speaking there are two types of illegality. A contract may be illegal because it involves the commission of a legal wrong. This legal wrong may be the aim of the contract or it may consist of the way in which the contract is performed. In some situations the mere fact that a particular contract was made amounts to a breach of law. The second kind of contracts which are illegal are contracts which are in some way against public policy. Obviously this can include a wide variety of different circumstances and not all types of illegality will be of the same seriousness.

4. Mistake

The concept of **mistake**, which exists both in common law and equity, is a difficult area of law. This is partly due to the fact that the classification of the different types of mistake and the terminology are not applied uniformly.

According to one classification there are three types of mistake. In the case of **unilateral mistake** one party has made a mistake of which the other party is aware. If both parties make exactly the same mistake it is called **common mistake.** In **mutual mistake** each party mistakes the intention of the other; they are at cross-purposes.

A second common classification of mistake distinguishes between mistake which **negatives consent** and mistake which **nullifies consent.** Consent is negatived if the mistake prevents the parties from reaching an agreement in the first place because they are at cross-purposes. If the parties reach an agreement that is based on a fundamental mistaken assumption, consent is nullified by the mistake.

For many years is was accepted that the effects of mistake depend on whether the rules of common law or of equity are applied. At common law the contract will be void *ab initio*, while in equity the contract is only voidable, and may be **rescinded on terms** by the court (*i.e.* the court may rectify the mistake). However, the Court of Appeal has questioned the ability of the courts to grant equitable relief where a contract is not void at common law, and it remains unclear whether this equitable jurisdiction still exists.

5. Misrepresentation

A **misrepresentation** is a false statement of past or existing fact made by one party before or at the time the contract is made, which is addressed to the other party and which induces the other party to enter into the contract. Misrepresentations must be distinguished from instances of **non-disclosure**. A person who is guilty of an active misrepresentation has said something that is not true, while in the case of non-disclosure someone has simply not volunteered information. The distinction is important because generally there is no **duty of disclosure** in English law.

A misrepresentation can be fraudulent, negligent or innocent, a distinction which refers to the state of mind of the representor. A misrepresentation is **fraudulent** if the representor knows that the statement he is making is false. If he is careless as to whether or not the representation is true he is guilty of a **negligent** misrepresentation. If the representor does not know, and could not reasonably know, that what he is saying is untrue the misrepresentation is said to be **innocent**. The remedies available to the representee depend on the kind of misrepresentation involved.

6. Duress and Undue Influence

Contracts are based on the agreement of the parties, they are based on consent. The concepts of duress and undue influence deal with situations in which a party has consented to a contract, but that consent is regarded as defective, because it was obtained by some form of pressure which the law regards as improper.

a) Duress

Duress is a common law concept which covers situations in which an illegitimate threat was used to force someone to enter into a contract. For a long time the requirement of 'threat' was given a very narrow interpretation; duress was restricted to cases of actual or threatened physical violence. It has now been recognised that physical violence is not the only kind of pressure that should be regarded as improper and the scope of duress has been widened considerably. The question which now has to be asked is whether the conduct in question was sufficient to constitute 'a coercion of the will which vitiates consent'.

Improper pressure which does not involve the threat of physical violence has become known as **economic duress**, and it is now well established that this is sufficient to constitute duress at common law. However, economic duress is not the same as commercial pressure. The threat involved must be illegitimate; the party exercising the pressure must do something more than just 'drive a hard bargain'.

b) Undue Influence

Undue influence is an equitable doctrine which provides relief where consent was obtained by some form of pressure which does not amount to duress at common law. In the case of **actual undue influence** it must be shown that such improper pressure existed on the facts of the case.

In certain situations the law presumes that undue influence was exercised because of the nature of the relationship between the parties. This type of undue influence is called **relational undue influence**. The relationship in question must be one of trust and confidence, which allows the dominant person to influence the judgment of the other. Relationships that automatically give rise to the presumption of undue influence include parent and child, doctor and patient, and solicitor and client. In other situations the weaker party must prove that their particular relationship was such that they were unable to exercise their free will.

VI. End of the Contract

1. Performance

Performance takes place when the parties fulfil their obligations under the contract. In order to discharge these obligations they must do exactly what they promised to do. Failure to perform will be a breach of contract, unless the party has an excuse for the failure, for example under the rules of frustration. A slight difference between what was promised and what was performed is sufficient to constitute a breach, even if it appears to be insignificant from a commercial point of view. Both **non-performance**, *i.e.* the failure to perform at all, and **malperformance**, *i.e.* the failure to perform correctly, amount to a breach of contract.

2. Breach

A party is in **breach** of contract if he does not want to or cannot fulfil his obligations under that contract without having a lawful excuse for his failure to perform. Generally a party who does not perform is not in breach of contract until his performance is due under the contract. Even before performance is due, however, a party can commit an **anticipatory breach** by indicating that he does not intend to perform his obligations at all. The same applies if a party incapacitates himself from performance, *i.e.* puts himself in a position in which he is unable to perform.

3. Frustration

The doctrine of **frustration** was developed to take account of the fact that events may occur after a contract has been formed which the parties could not foresee and which in some way interfere with performance, for example because the subject-matter of the contract has been destroyed. Under this doctrine both parties may be discharged from their obligations under a contract, if after its formation events occur which change the circumstances so much that performance becomes impossible or illegal.

Frustration applies only to events which are not due to the fault of either party and which were not provided for in the contract. The fact that performance has become more onerous for one party is not sufficient to invoke this doctrine.

VII. Remedies

1. Damages

The main remedy for breach of contract in English law is an action for **damages**, *i.e.* **monetary compensation**. The aim of contractual damages is compensation of the claimant for the fact that he has not received what is due to him under the contract, not punishment of the defendant.

Damages are **available as of right** whenever a contract has been broken. The claimant only has to show that a breach has occurred, he does not have to prove that he has in fact suffered a loss. Obviously the amount of damages awarded will depend on the actual loss of the claimant; if he has not suffered any he will receive only nominal damages.

2. Specific Performance

Specific performance is an equitable remedy and as all such remedies is discretionary only. The court orders the defaulting party to fulfil his obligations under the contract. Specific performance is only granted when damages are inadequate to compensate the claimant for the loss he has suffered.

3. Restitution

Restitution is ordered when one party has performed all or part of his obligations without receiving the counter-performance. Where the performed obligation consisted of the payment of a sum of money the same amount will be returned to the claimant. If some other benefit was conferred onto the defendant, the claimant is entitled to receive a sum equivalent to the value of that benefit.

VIII. Terminology

Condition: the word condition has several different meanings. Generally a condition is a prerequisite for something else – something that must happen for a right to exist. If a contract is said to be **conditional,** its existence depends on the occurrence (or non-occurrence) of an event. In this context there are two forms of conditions: **condition precedent** means that existence of the contract is delayed until the occurrence of a specified event; **condition subsequent** means that the contract exists until a specified event occurs. The opposite of a conditional contract is an **unconditional contract.** However, in the text condition has a different meaning. It can also refer to the **classification** of the terms of a contract. A condition is a term of the contract, breach of which entitles the innocent party to claim damages and terminate the agreement. In this context conditions can be contrasted with warranties and innominate terms.

Consideration: in this context it does not mean deliberation or thought. It means that something of legal value must be given to the other party to make their promise binding; consideration is the element of reciprocity required in English contract law. The term refers both to that which is actually given in return for a promise, and to the doctrine as a whole.

Damages: it is very important to distinguish between **damage** and **damages.** Damage is loss, injury or harm (whether to a person or property); it is always used in the singular. Damages refers to monetary compensation which one person has to pay to another to make up for damage caused; in this meaning it is always used in the plural.

Intermediate / innominate terms: terms in a contract which are neither conditions nor warranties; they lie between the two (hence the name intermediate terms). They have no separate characteristics, but instead assume the features of either conditions or warranties, depending on the facts of the case (hence the name innominate terms). If the breach of an innominate term is so serious as to entitle to other party to terminate the contract, it is treated like a condition; if the other party can only claim damages, it is treated like a warranty.

Legally enforceable: if one party fails to perform his obligations under the contract, the other party can obtain legal redress. It should be noted that this does not always mean that the party in breach will be forced to perform; the main remedy for breach of contract is damages.

Misrepresentation: a representation in contract law is something said by either party before or at the time the contract is formed (in this context it does not refer to the representation of one person by another). A misrepresentation is not simply a statement made by either party which is untrue; it must be a false statement of fact which induces the other party to enter into the contract.

Offeror / offeree: the ending '-or' denotes that a person is active, giving or doing something, while '-ee' denotes someone who is passive, who receives something. Thus the offeror is the person making an offer, while the offeree is the person receiving that offer. The same applies to promisor (person making a promise) and promisee (person receiving a promise), and to **representor** (person making a representation) and **representee** (person receiving a representation).

Performance: takes place when one party does what he promised to do under the contract; it does not have to be a positive act.

Principal: the person on whose behalf an agent is acting. This word must not be confused with **principle**.

Promissor / promisee: see offeror / offeree.

Reciprocity: a mutually beneficial exchange.

Rescind: to set a voidable contract aside. **Rescission** means that the parties are treated as if the contract had never existed.

IX. Review and Discussion

1. ***Explain the terms valid consideration, sufficient consideration, adequate consideration and nominal consideration.***

Under the doctrine of consideration a promise is only binding if something is given in return for it. Anything which, if given to the other party, makes a promise binding is called good and therefore valid consideration. The term sufficient consideration is used in contrast with adequate consideration. It means that whatever is given in return for a promise must have some value in the eye of the law, it must be sufficient. However, it need not have the same economic value as that for which it is exchanged, it need not be adequate. Therefore a promise to give £50 in return for a car worth £1000 is binding, although the two things do not have the same economic value. The principle that consideration must be sufficient but need not be adequate means that even nominal consideration can be valid. Nominal consideration is consideration that has no real economic value, or a value that is so small as to be negligible. A common example is a peppercorn (hence the term 'peppercorn consideration'). Pepper certainly has an economic value, but the value of an individual corn is very small. Nevertheless it can constitute valid consideration.

2. ***What are the essential elements of a legally enforceable contract?***

There must be an offer and an acceptance, consideration, the intention to create legal relations and compliance with formal requirements (if there are any).

3. What is the difference between duress and undue influence?

There are several differences between duress and undue influence. Firstly, duress is a common law concept, undue influence is an equitable doctrine. Secondly, undue influence is wider, in that it covers forms of behaviour which are regarded as wrongful, but do not amount to duress. Thirdly, duress must always be proven by the person claiming to have been pressurised; undue influence can be presumed in certain circumstances, and it is then up to the party alleged to have exercised the undue influence to show that this did not in fact happen.

4. Explain the following terms: mirror image rule, counter-offer, invitation to treat.

Under the **mirror image rule** the acceptance must correspond exactly with the terms of the offer, it must be its mirror image. If, for example, A offers his car to B for £5000, B must agree to buy it for that amount. If B tells A that he will buy the car for £4000, his intended acceptance does not correspond with the offer, and no contract is formed. B has actually not accepted A's offer at all; instead he has made a **counter-offer**. This means that he has made a new offer, which A (who is now the offeree) can either accept or reject. This counter-offer destroys the original offer. If A refuses to sell for £4000 B cannot suddenly change his mind and try to buy the car for £5000; he must wait until A makes another offer.

An offer must be distinguished from a mere **invitation to treat**. An invitation to treat is a statement that invites another person to make an offer. Such a statement cannot be turned into a binding contract by simple acceptance. A common example of an invitation to treat is the display of goods in a shop window. The offer is made by the person who takes the goods to the cash desk; the owner of the shop can decide whether to accept or reject this offer.

5. What are the main pieces of legislation controlling express terms in contracts?

The **Unfair Contract Terms Act 1977** deals primarily with exemption clauses. Some clauses are rendered completely ineffective by the statute (for example a party to a contract cannot exclude liability for negligently causing death or personal injury), while others are valid only to the extent that they are reasonable. The **Unfair Terms in Consumer Contracts Regulations 1999** are wider in their application, because they apply to all terms in a contract between a seller and a consumer that have not been individually negotiated (*i.e.* standard form contracts). The test applied by the Regulations (and the EC Directive pursuant to which they were enacted) is that of fairness. A term is unfair if, contrary to the requirement of good faith, it leads to a significant imbalance in the parties' rights and obligations to the detriment of the consumer.

6. What is assignment?

Assignment is the transfer of rights under a contract by a party to that contract (the **assignor**) to a third party (the **assignee**). The consent of the other party to the contract is not required. The assignee can then enforce those rights against the other party. Assignment can take place under statutory provisions, or as equitable assignment.

Chapter 11: The Law of Tort

I. Introduction

A **tort** is a civil wrong independent of contract. Although this definition has the advantage of brevity, it lacks precision. Indeed, the **law of tort** is difficult to define, which is why in the following emphasis will be placed on description, rather than definition. Tort law covers a wide variety of different situations. X is careless while driving his car and causes an accident in which Y is injured; X writes a newspaper article in which he falsely accused Y of being a thief; X enters Y's property without permission. Each of these scenarios amounts to a different tort (negligence, defamation and trespass respectively). What they have in common is that X has behaved in a way that the law regards as wrongful. It is the function of the law of tort to provide a remedy in such situations by allowing Y, the injured party, to bring a civil action against X, the **tortfeasor**.

Tort law must be distinguished from criminal law and the law of contract. Breach of contract, like a tort, is a civil wrong. This means that the innocent party can initiate civil proceedings against the defaulting party. The difference between tort and contract law is that **liability** in contract law requires a pre-existing contractual relationship between the parties, while there is no need for any prior connection between people involved in a tort case. Criminal law differs from the law of tort in that the action is brought by the state in the criminal courts, with the aim of punishing an offender. An action in tort law is brought by the victim in the civil courts and a remedy is provided to compensate the claimant for the loss he has suffered. However, there is also some overlap between the different areas. **Concurrent liability** in tort and contract can exist if a breach of contract results in, for example, physical injury to the other party; behaviour which gives rise to **tortious liability** can also amount to a crime.

II. Fundamental Principles of Tortious Liability

1. Introduction

Every tort has its own constitutive elements, which the claimant must establish before he can recover damages. *Prima facie* what is required is a wrongful act by the defendant and damage suffered by the claimant. However, this is not enough and the claimant may still fail on the issues of causation and remoteness, or he may be found **guilty** of contributory negligence. This principle can defeat a claim, regardless of how wrongful the defendant's act was and how much damage the claimant suffered.

Questions of causation, remoteness and contributory negligence can be relevant in relation to all torts, but they arise most commonly in cases of negligence.

2. Causation

Causation means that the claimant must establish a **causal link** between the defendant's behaviour and the damage he has suffered; in most cases he must show that, had the other person not acted as he did, the loss or injury would not have occurred. The question is whether, but for the defendant's action, the claimant would have been injured; it is therefore known as the **'but-for test'** of causation. The defendant is only **liable** for the damage he has actually caused.

In many cases the issue of causation will be straightforward, but two situations have caused particular difficulties in recent years. The first concerns a claimant who was not, for example, properly informed about all the risks involved in an operation. It will often be impossbile to prove that, had the correct information been provided, the claimant would definitely have chosen not to undergo the procedure; but showing that the claimant would have sought further advice, or taken more time to decide, does not fulfil the criteria of the but-for test. In a recent case the House of Lords departed from the standard test based on policy considerations, but it has been made clear that this was an exception. The second problematic area concerns industrial illnesses, such as those caused by the inhalation of coal dust or asbestos. These medical conditions usually take years, if not decades, to develop, during which time the claimant may well have worked for different employers. It has been held that here a claimant need only show that a particular employer **materially contributed** to the risk in order to recover a proportion of the damages.

3. Remoteness

Any act of a person can set in motion a chain of events that can lead to almost unlimited consequences. For purely practical reasons no defendant will be held liable for everything that happens as a result of his behaviour; liability must be limited in time and space. Consequences that are too indirect, too far removed from the original act are said to be too **remote**. The claimant will not be able to recover damages. **Remoteness** is a judicial control device to restrict unlimited liability on the basis of practicality rather than logic. It is therefore also referred to as **legal causation**.

4. Contributory Negligence

Even where the defendant's act has been established as a cause of the damage, it may not be the only cause. The law on **contributory negligence** acknowledges that the claimant may himself be partly responsible for the damage he has suffered, if he himself acted negligently. A clear example is the claimant who is injured in a road traffic accident caused by the defendant. If the defendant can show that the injuries would have been less severe if the claimant had fastened his seat belt, the claimant will be guilty of contributory negligence. Under the **Law Reform (Contributory Negligence) Act 1945** damages will be **apportioned** according to the **culpability** of each party. Thus, if the injuries would have been half as severe if the claimant had fastened his seat belt, he will only receive 50 percent of the damages.

III. Main Torts

1. Defamation

A person who publishes an untrue statement that reflects negatively on another's **reputation** commits the tort of **defamation**. It is not sufficient that the person concerned feels offended by the publication; it must lower him in the estimation of right-thinking members of society. A statement will also be **defamatory** if it leads to a person being shunned or avoided by others. There are two forms of defamation, depending on the way in which the statement is published.

Libel refers to defamatory representations made in a permanent form, such as writing, printing and pictures. It therefore covers books, newspapers and other printed matter and has been extended by statute to include radio and television broadcasts and theatrical performances. In contrast, **slander** is the conveyance of a defamatory meaning through spoken words or gestures.

Unlike most civil actions, defamation cases are often heard before a jury. Although there is normally no measurable financial loss to the claimant, **awards** of damages have been increasingly extravagant, prompting calls for the removal of juries from such cases.

2. Nuisance

Nuisances are divided into private nuisance and public nuisance. There is some degree of overlap, in that the same conduct can amount to both, but it is important to maintain the distinction. A private nuisance is a tort, whereas a public nuisance is a crime.

a) Private Nuisance

A **private nuisance** is the unreasonable interference with the reasonable enjoyment of land. The defendant does something (or omits to do something) which disturbs the claimant in the use of his property. The interference might cause physical damage to the land (for example if poisonous emissions from the defendant's factory kill the plants in the claimant's garden), or it might disturb the claimant's enjoyment of the land (for example if loud music from next door prevents him from sleeping). The disturbance can take a variety of forms: smoke, smells, overhanging branches and noise are but a few examples of what may constitute a nuisance.

At the heart of the law on nuisance lies the balancing of conflicting interests, the claimant's right to peaceful enjoyment of his land on the one hand, and the defendant's right to carry out certain activities on the other. The court will look at a number of different factors, such as the location of the property (something which is permissible in one place may amount to a nuisance somewhere else), the type of injury suffered by the claimant (physical damage is more serious than intangible damage) and the reasonableness of the defendant's conduct.

b) Public Nuisance

A **public nuisance** is an act or omission which materially affects the reasonable comfort and convenience of life of a class of Her Majesty's subjects. A common example is the obstruction of a **highway** by the defendant, the relevant class of people being all those who are prevented from using that road. Unlike private nuisance, public nuisance is not limited to interference with land and can include such things as the selling of food unfit for human consumption.

Creation of a public nuisance will normally result in a criminal prosecution being brought against the person responsible. An individual cannot bring a private action against the defendant, unless he can show that he has suffered some special damage, *i.e.* that his loss is greater than that caused to others who are affected by the nuisance. However, the Attorney-General may bring a civil action on behalf of a member of the public, a so-called **relator action**.

3. Trespass

Originally **trespass** simply meant 'wrong'. Today it is a tort which can be committed against a person, to land or to goods.

Trespass to goods occurs where one person intentionally and forcefully interferes with goods possessed by another person. The goods in question need not be owned by the claimant but merely possessed, and trespass in this sense may be committed by merely touching goods possessed by another. For example, a painting hanging in a museum may be owned by an art collector but possessed by the museum in order to show it. If a visitor to the gallery intentionally and without permission touches the painting he can be said to have committed the tort of trespass against the gallery.

Trespass to land is the unjustifiable interference with the possession of land. Thus a person who enters property belonging to another without permission is a **trespasser.** In some circumstances trespass can amount to a crime (for example in the form of **aggravated trespass**), but normally it is a tort only. It should therefore be noted that the commonly displayed sign "trespassers will be prosecuted" is wrong – in most cases trespasser can be sued, but not prosecuted.

There are three main forms of **trespass to the person**, all of which amount to crimes as well as torts. **Battery** can be described as the intentional and direct application of **force** to another person. 'Force' here includes any physical contact that is unwanted by the recipient; it does not have to be violent. An **assault** is an act done by the defendant which causes a person to apprehend that force will be used against him. An attack on an individual will often include both assault and battery, but they can be committed independently of each other. Thus where X goes to strike Y, but then does not, this is an assault without battery; if X attacks Y from behind this is battery without assault. Finally, the infliction of bodily restraint that is not expressly or impliedly authorised by law is called **false imprisonment.** This tort does not require imprisonment of a person in the usual sense; there does not have to be any physical contact between the tortfeasor and the victim, nor need there be a prison. It is sufficient that the victim is completely deprived of his liberty in some way.

Trespass is an exception to the general rules of tort law, in that the claimant need not show that he has actually suffered any damage: trespass is **actionable per se.** The mere fact that a trespass has occurred is sufficient to bring an action, although of course the claimant may only receive **nominal damages**, if he has not actually suffered any loss.

4. Strict Liability: The Rule in Rylands v Fletcher

Generally **strict liability** refers to a system where liability is imposed even though a person did not act intentionally or negligently. It is therefore an exception to the general rule that tortious liability is based on **fault.** Strict liability exists in relation to several torts (such as breach of a statutory duty), but it has also developed into a separate principle in relation to land. This principle is often called the **rule in *Rylands v Fletcher***, after the case in which it was established (reported at (1868) L.R. 3 H.L. 330). A person who collects on his land something which is likely to cause harm if it escapes, is **strictly liable** for any damage caused by an escape. It does not matter whether the escape was his fault or not; the mere fact that damage has been caused by something which came from his land means that he is responsible. A remarkably wide variety of things has been held to be potentially dangerous according to this rule, including water, fire, gas, electricity and poisonous vegetation. These examples show that there is a close link between the rule in *Rylands v Fletcher* and the law on nuisance, but strict liability is usually regarded as a separate principle.

5. Negligence

The word **negligence** has several distinct meanings in the law of tort. First, it can refer to a person's state of mind; in this context it is the opposite of **intention**. The tort of trespass, for example, can be committed **intentionally** (if X intends to step onto Y's property without permission) or **negligently** (if X does not think about whether he is allowed to enter a piece of land). Secondly, it can simply be a synonym for **careless** conduct, such as when a person closes a door but does not check whether it is properly locked. Thirdly, negligence can mean a separate tort and it is this meaning which is relevant here. In practical terms negligence is perhaps the most important tort, and a large number of cases are brought each year in which one person claims to have suffered damage or loss through the negligence of another.

The tort of negligence involves more than just carelessness. It is the breach of a **legal duty to take care**, which is imposed on the defendant *vis-à-vis* the claimant. There are therefore three questions that must be answered in the affirmative before a defendant will be found liable. First of all, did the defendant owe the claimant a legal duty to take care? In some areas the existence of such a duty is well-established; a motorist, for example, is under a clear obligation not to harm other road-users. In other situations it is not so easy to decide whether a legal duty should be imposed. The courts have found it difficult to formulate a general test of liability which could simply be applied to novel circumstances, and there are always many different factors and considerations that must be taken into account.

Once it is clear that a **duty of care** exists between both parties, the question is whether the defendant is **in breach** of that duty. This will be the case if he has failed to attain the **standard of care** that the law requires of him. The test is objective, the standard is that of the **reasonable person**. A person is **negligent** if he does something that a reasonable person would not do, or if he omits to do something that a reasonable person would do. Again it is not possible to formulate a simple test; the court will look at a variety of factors and decide whether, on the facts of the case, the defendant acted **negligently**. The final question is whether the defendant's negligence caused damage to the claimant. It is at this stage that issues of causation and remoteness will be relevant.

The law on negligence is in many areas vague and imprecise. This is due to the nature of the subject. Negligent behaviour can occur in different ways, there are many different types of relationship between people that may or may not give rise to a duty of care and there are numerous other variables in each case. In addition, a negligent act can cause different forms of damage, which are governed by distinct rules. The most straightforward kinds of damage (as far as legal consequences are concerned) are **personal injury** and **property damage**.

Physical damage is (relatively) easy to quantify and there are no public policy considerations against holding a defendant liable for all damage to persons or property that he has caused. **Economic loss** and **nervous shock** have proved more problematic. Nervous shock is the legal term for **psychiatric illness** suffered as a result of the defendant's negligence. It is increasingly recognised that this type of harm can be as serious as physical injury, and recovery of damages is possible, provided that the claimant is suffering from a medically recognisable illness. Mere grief and emotional upset are not sufficient to warrant an award of damages. Problems have arisen in respect of so-called **secondary victims**, *i.e.* persons who are not directly affected by the negligent act, but who suffer nervous shock when they are, for example, told about an accident that has occurred. Fears over the number of potential secondary victims have led to restrictions being imposed on the basis of public policy.

Similar concerns over the proper limit of liability arise in relation to economic loss. **Financial loss** suffered by the claimant will normally be directly linked to property damage, for example where a taxi driver claims for lost income, because his taxi was damaged by the defendant. There is a causal link between property damage and financial loss. In cases of **pure economic loss** there is no such causal link, the damage is not directly attributable to property damage or personal injury. A clear example is the situation in which a person relies on negligent advice given to him by another, as a result of which he suffers financial loss. There is no connection between the loss and any physical damage; the advisor is guilty of negligence, and he has caused a loss, but there is no tangible damage. This example also illustrates the main problem in relation to economic loss, namely the issue of proper limitation of liability. A negligent act which causes pure economic loss will often affect many more people than one which results in property damage. Considerations of practicability and public policy have therefore resulted in a restriction of circumstances in which recovery for pure economic loss will be possible.

IV. Remedies

1. Introduction

The two main remedies available to the victim of a tort are **damages** and **injunctions**. Of these damages are by far the most important in practical terms. Injunctions are dealt with in detail elsewhere; for present purposes it will suffice to indicate the type of situation in which an injunction might be an appropriate remedy against a tortfeasor.

The tort of trespass is actionable per se; this means that the claimant can bring an action against the defendant without proof of any damage. If X repeatedly trespasses onto Y's property without causing any damage, Y can bring an action for each trespass, but he will only be awarded nominal damages. This remedy is of little use to him, as it does not stop X from trespassing. An injunction, on the other hand, will order X to stop; if he fails to comply he will be in contempt of court, an offence punishable by imprisonment. This remedy is likely to be much more effective in stopping the trespass than nominal damages.

2. Damages

Damages are the amount of money that the defendant is ordered to pay to the claimant once he has been found liable. The aim is to compensate the claimant for the loss he has suffered; to the extent that this is possible through financial means the claimant is to be placed in the position he would have been in if the tort had not occurred. Thus, if the defendant has caused £1000 worth of damage to the claimant's car, he will have to pay £1000 in damages. Assessment of the amount payable is a little more complex in personal injury cases, but established **heads of damage** provide a certain degree of predictability. The damage suffered by the victim is roughly divided into **pecuniary** and **non-pecuniary**

loss. The former covers things like **loss of earnings** and **medical expenses**, while the latter encompasses **pain and suffering** and **loss of amenities**.

Most awards of damages are intended to be purely compensatory; the objective is to **indemnify** the claimant, not punish the defendant. In rare cases, however, the court may award **exemplary** or **punitive damages** in order to punish the defendant and to deter him from behaving in a similar way in the future. Such damages will be appropriate if the defendant has, for example, calculated that the profit he stands to make will exceed the likely amount of damages. Exemplary damages ensure that he does not gain a benefit from his tortious behaviour.

V. Defences

1. Introduction

Even if the claimant succeeds in establishing the necessary elements of a tort, he may fail in his action if the defendant can rely on a **defence**, that is a legally recognised excuse or justification for his conduct. A **complete defence** will free the defendant from all liability, while a **partial defence**, such as contributory negligence, only reduces the amount of damages payable. Some defences apply to all torts, others are only available in relation to specific torts. The former are called **general**, the latter **special defences**.

2. General Defences

One of the most important defences is that of **consent**, often expressed in the Latin formula ***volenti non fit injuria***. The claimant cannot bring an action in tort if he has consented to the conduct in question. A boxer who agrees to a fight cannot sue his opponent for assault and battery if he is hit, even though such an attack would certainly be tortious if it occurred in different circumstances. By taking part in a particular sporting activity he consents to all types of conduct that are within the rules of the sport in question, and takes the risk that injury might occur.

The defence of ***ex turpi causa non oritur actio*** or **illegality** is available where the injury arises while both parties are engaged in an illegal activity. Thus X cannot sue Y if he is injured as a result of Y's negligence during a joint burglary. This defence is based on public policy; it is regarded as undesirable that a person should be able to sue in circumstances where his own illegal behaviour cannot be separated from the tort.

In some circumstances it might be necessary to cause some degree of damage, in order to avoid greater loss. If X trespasses onto Y's property in order to extinguish a fire, or pulls down a building in order to prevent the spread of flames, he can raise the defence of **necessity**, because, even though his action caused some damage, greater loss would have resulted from his inactivity.

3. Special Defences

It is not possible in this context to list all special defences that are available for individual torts, therefore only a few examples will be given.

The law on defamation recognises that in some circumstances **freedom of speech** is more important than the protection of an individual's reputation. Such communications, for example statements made in parliamentary debate or during judicial proceedings, are therefore protected by **privilege**. This means that an action cannot be brought in respect of them, even though they might in fact be defamatory.

A claim for trespass to land can be defeated if the defendant had permission to enter the property in question, a so-called **licence**. A further defence, namely that of **justification by law**, is available to people like police officers, who may enter premises in order to arrest someone.

Even strict liability may be evaded if the defendant can rely on the defence of ***vis major***, otherwise known as **Act of God**. This applies when the event that caused the escape could not have been prevented by the defendant because it was the act of a greater power, *i.e.* a natural catastrophe, such as a flood or an earthquake.

VI. Terminology

Assault and battery: two distinct torts; however, the term assault is often used to refer to both actions.

***Ex turpi causa non oritur actio*:** literally 'no action can be based on a disreputable cause'.

Exemplary damages: must not be confused with **aggravated damages**. The aim of exemplary damages is to punish the defendant for his conduct. Aggravated damages are purely compensatory; they are awarded where the claimant's injury has been increased by the defendant's malicious or oppressive behaviour, for example where a trespass is committed in a particularly objectionable manner. Although there is a clear conceptual difference between the two types of damages, they can be difficult to distinguish in individual cases.

Guilty: a person is often said to be 'guilty' of a tort (for example 'guilty of negligence'). This must not be confused with 'guilty' in the criminal sense; a tort is a civil wrong, and although certain things can be both a crime and a tort, criminal liability must be established separately. A person who is said to be guilty of a tort will not necessarily also be guilty of a crime.

Highway: a road or way which is open to the public; it can be on land or water, thus including streets, paths, bridges and rivers.

Law of tort: some people prefer the term **law of torts**, as the law is not based on a single principle of liability, but a number of distinct torts.

Liability: legal obligation. A person found to be liable for a wrong such as a tort or a breach of contract is held responsible for it; this encompasses an obligation to repair any damage caused.

Loss of amenity: also called **loss of enjoyment of life**, referring to the reduction or loss of the claimant's ability to do things that he used to do. Thus if, for example, he can no longer participate in a sport or other hobby, this will be included in the assessment of damages.

Material contribution: where an act or omission is a substantial and operative cause of a claimant's damage that significantly increased the risk of damage occurring.

Negligence: it is very important always to distinguish between 'negligence' as a state of mind and 'negligence' as an independent tort. The former is synonymous with carelessness, inadvertence and lack of diligence. In the latter, a person's state of mind is irrelevant; it is his conduct that is judged. Thus, if X drives too fast and causes an accident, he will be guilty of negligence. He has breached his duty of care towards others, even if he was concentrating and paid full attention to the road.

Nominal damages: when the claimant has shown that his right has been infringed in some way, but has not been able to show that he has actually suffered any damage, the court will award a very small amount of money (for example £1) as nominal damages. The aim is not to compensate the claimant, but to acknowledge that the defendant has committed a tort.

Reasonable person: also referred to as the **reasonable man**. The objective standard of reasonableness plays an important part in many areas of law; the hypothetical reasonable person is the personification of this abstract standard.

***Rylands v Fletcher*:** (1868) L.R. 3 H.L. 330 is an old law report.

VII. Review and Discussion

1. Which interests are protected by the law of tort?

The law of tort is aimed at the protection of three main interests, namely a person's physical integrity, his property and his reputation. Thus a claimant will receive compensation if he has suffered personal injury or property damage through the defendant's negligence; the law on trespass to land, nuisance and the rule in *Rylands v Fletcher* safeguards both the physical integrity and an individual's enjoyment of his property; and defamation deals with injury to reputation. There are two kinds of damage which do not fit into this system: nervous shock and pure economic loss. Psychiatric injury is now recognised as being akin to physical injury, thus making recovery possible. Pure economic loss, however, remains outside the interests which are traditionally protected by tort law, and damages will only be awarded in limited circumstances.

2. What are the key elements of negligence as an independent tort?

In order to establish a claim for negligence the claimant must prove that the defendant owed him a duty of care, that he was in breach of this duty, and that this breach resulted in damage to the claimant.

The existence of a legal duty of care depends on a variety of factors. Generally it can be said that a duty will exist if it is foreseeable that the claimant will be affected by the defendant's conduct. However, policy factors also play an important part at this stage. The question whether someone has in fact acted negligently is decided by reference to the hypothetical reasonable person. The defendant will have breached his duty of care if he acted in a way which is regarded as unreasonable. The final element of negligence raises issues of causation and remoteness. The claimant must prove that there is a causal link between the defendant's action and the damage he has suffered. This is done by applying the so-called 'but-for' test: if the claimant would not have suffered any damage but for the defendant's negligence, causation is established (there are a small number of exceptional cases where a different test of causation is applied). Remoteness is a control device at the end of the process, employed by the courts to limit liability. If the consequences of an action are too far removed from the original occurrence the defendant will not be liable.

3. *What is the neighbour principle?*

The so-called **neighbour principle** lies at the heart of the tort of negligence. It was established by Lord Atkin in the case of *Donoghue v Stevenson* [1932] A.C. 562, the first case to recognise a general duty of care. Prior to this decision, negligence was only recognised in relation to particular circumstances, such as road accidents. *Donoghue v Stevenson* represents the first attempt by the courts to formulate a general principle of liability, intended to cover all possible situations. It was held that a person owes a duty of care to his neighbour. This statement on its own is not hugely helpful, so Lord Atkin went on to explain that someone is a 'neighbour' if it is **reasonably foreseeable** that he will be affected by the conduct in question.

This principle certainly has the advantage of simplicity, being based, as it is, on reasonable foresight only. However, it has become clear that it is far too wide to operate successfully and there are situations where the mere fact that damage to the claimant was reasonably foreseeable is not sufficient to impose liability on the defendant. There are a number of different factors that a court must take into account when deciding whether a duty of care exists in a particular situation, including policy considerations. There is no simple test of liability that can be applied to novel circumstances.

4. *What factors will a court look at in order to decide whether a person has acted negligently?*

The general criterion for judging the behaviour of the defendant is the reasonable person. This standard is abstract and difficult to define, because what is reasonable depends on the circumstances; the characteristics of the reasonable man will vary with the circumstances of each case. Generally it can be said that he is ordinary, typical; he is neither particularly courageous, nor particularly timid; neither reckless nor over-careful; neither an expert in law nor totally without common sense.

In trying to apply this hypothetical being to a particular case the court will look at a variety of factors, to decide whether the conduct in question was reasonable. First, there is the magnitude of the risk. The more likely it is that something will happen, the more precautions will be deemed necessary (and therefore reasonable). Closely linked to this is the second factor, the seriousness of the potential injury. If something is unlikely to happen (the first factor), but it is known that if it does occur damage will be severe, then again greater efforts must be made to avoid the event. Thirdly, the court will have regard to the importance of what the defendant was doing at the time when the claimant was injured. If he was engaged in an activity of high social value, he is less likely to be considered negligent. Thus an ambulance driver responding to an emergency call is justified in taking higher risks than someone who is driving to work. Finally, the practicability of precautions must be taken into account. Many car accidents could be avoided if the maximum speed limit was five miles per hour, but this would not be very practicable. If it is very easy to safeguard against a particular risk, the defendant will be expected to do so. What exactly amounts to 'reasonable precautions' again depends to a significant degree on the magnitude and nature of the risk involved.

Chapter 12: Commercial Law

I. Commercial Law

The term **'commercial law'** covers a wide range of individual areas of law, which have in common that they concern the relationships which arise in the course of business transactions. This includes (but is not limited to) the law relating to contracts for the **carriage** and **insurance** of goods, **banking law**, **agency** and of course the paradigm of commercial law, the **sale and supply of goods**. Contract law lies at the heart of all these areas, and the general rules of contracting apply. In addition, however, the specialist nature of each has led to the development of distinct principles. As it is not possible to deal with all these aspects of commercial law in this context, the following discussion will concentrate on sale of goods law.

II. Introduction to Sale of Goods Law

1. Definition of Contract of Sale

Sale of goods law has been regulated by statute for a considerable time. The first Sale of Goods Act was enacted in 1893 and consolidated by the **Sale of Goods Act 1979** (**SGA 1979**). The present law must be sought in this 1979 Act as amended over time, for example by the **Sale and Supply of Goods Act 1994** and the **Sale of Goods (Amendment) Act 1995**. It should be noted that the SGA 1979 covers both commercial and **consumer contracts**. Although there are an increasing number of individual rules that are specific to consumer contracts, such as those introduced by the **Sale and Supply of Goods to Consumers Regulations 2002**, the basic principles are the same.

The SGA 1979 applies only to **contracts for the sale of goods**. Such a contract is defined as one by which the seller transfers or agrees to transfer the property in goods to the buyer for a money consideration, called the **price**. A distinction is drawn between contracts under which property in the goods is transferred from seller to buyer, called **sale**, and contracts under which this transfer is to take place at a future time, called **agreement to sell**. As will be seen below it is important that the consideration provided by the buyer is money, but it does not matter whether the price is paid immediately (sale for **cash**) or whether the buyer promises to pay at a later date (sale for **credit**). The parties to a contract of sale are the **seller**, the person who sells or agrees to sell, and the **buyer**, who buys or agrees to buy goods.

Contracts of sale must be distinguished from other legal relationships. The distinction is not always easy, but it is important, because the provisions of the SGA 1979 apply only to agreements that fall within the definition of a contract of sale.

A **gift** is the transfer of property without consideration. Under the general rules of contract law the promise of a gift is only binding if it is made in a deed. In most cases it is not difficult to distinguish between a gift and a contract of sale, but problems have arisen in cases in which a 'free gift' was offered to buyers on the purchase of certain (or a certain amount of) goods. In such a case the 'free gift' might be a true gift, or it might be the subject-matter of a **collateral contract**.

The statutory definition of a contract of sale clearly states that the consideration provided by the buyer must be money. Therefore any contract under which the seller delivers goods in exchange for other goods or for services is not a contract of sale, but a contract of **barter** or **exchange**. The rules laid down in the SGA 1979 do not apply to such contracts.

A contract of **bailment** is an agreement under which goods are delivered by one person, called **bailor**, to another, called **bailee**, for a limited purpose; the bailee is required to hold the goods and to return them to the bailor when instructed to do so. A typical example of bailment is that of a person who puts his coat in a cloakroom, to be kept there until he returns. The parties do not intend property to pass, and the bailee does not become the owner when the goods are delivered to him.

A **hire-purchase agreement** is a contract for the hiring of goods which at the same time confers on the buyer an **option** to buy the goods. The buyer has the choice whether or not to buy the goods; he is not obliged to do so. This is an important difference between contracts of sale and hire-purchase agreements, as under a contract of sale the buyer is obliged to complete the sale. The goods which are subject to the hire-purchase agreement remain the property of the original owner, unless and until the buyer exercises his option to buy. In practice most hire-purchase contracts look very much like contracts of sale, because the real aim of the transaction is the sale of the goods in question. The use of a hire-purchase agreement allows the buyer to use the goods before the full price has been paid, while the seller retains ownership as security against non-payment. Despite the similarities, however, the legal distinction between sale and hire-purchase should be maintained.

Agency is a relationship under which one person, the **agent**, is authorised to act as a representative of another, the **principal**. It is important to distinguish between agency and a contract of sale, because different rules apply to these transactions. However, it is not always easy to make this distinction. If, for example, party A has been asked by party B to obtain goods from a third party, and A does deliver these goods to B, he may be acting as B's agent or he may be selling B the goods which he himself bought from the third party. In the first case the relationship between A and B is that of principal and agent, in the second case it is a contract of sale.

It is often very difficult to distinguish between a contract of sale and a **contract for services**, as contracts for the performance of work often include the supply of materials or other goods. A painter agrees to paint a portrait – is he entering into a contract for services (the actual work of painting) or is he selling a picture under a contract of sale? In many cases it does not matter into which category a particular agreement falls, because the same rules apply to contracts of sale and contracts for services. However, where the distinction needs to be drawn it has to be based on the question whether the provision of services or the goods themselves form the substance of the contract.

2. Subject-Matter of the Contract

a) Definition of 'Goods'

It might at first glance seem easy to determine what can be the subject-matter of a contract of sale, *i.e.* what constitutes **'goods'**. However, the statutory definition is rather specific, and it is necessary to be aware of what is, and what is not, covered by it. 'Goods' includes all **personal chattels** other than **things in action** and money. **Chattels** are all property other than land. They can be divided into **chattels real** and chattels personal. The former are interests which are connected to land (such as leases) and do not constitute 'goods', while the latter are tangible goods, so-called **movables**. These can again be subdivided into **choses** (or **things**) **in possession** and **choses** (or **things**) **in action**. Choses in possession are things which can be seen, touched and moved, such as household articles, clothes, bicycles, domestic animals and everything that can be physically transferred from one place to another. Money is also a chose in possession, but it is expressly excluded from the definition of 'goods' for the purposes of sales law. Choses in action, on the other hand, are intangible. They include copyrights and patents, debts, **negotiable instruments** and insurance policies. Choses in action can be transferred from one person to another, but these transactions are not contracts of sale.

b) Classification of Goods

Goods which form the subject-matter of a contract of sale can be of various kinds. First, they may be either **existing** or **future** goods. Existing goods are goods which are owned or possessed by the seller, while goods which are yet to be manufactured or acquired by him are future goods. A third type, which is not mentioned in the SGA 1979, is the **spes**. The buyer takes the chance, *i.e.* the risk that the goods come into existence, for example by agreeing to pay a fixed price for the crop of a particular field. He will have to pay, even if little or no goods are in fact produced, while the seller is only obliged to deliver goods that actually come into existence.

A second important distinction has to be drawn between **specific** and **unascertained** goods. Specific goods are goods which are identified and agreed on at the time the contract of sale is made. Unascertained goods are not defined in the Act, but must logically be goods that are not identified and agreed on at that time. Goods which are identified by the parties after the contract is made are called **ascertained goods**. The distinction between specific and unascertained goods is important in relation to the question when property in the goods passes to the buyer, as different rules apply to the two kinds of goods.

III. Duties of the Seller

1. Duty to Pass Good Title

The ultimate aim of a contract of sale is that **title** to the goods should pass from seller to buyer. 'Title' is here used as a synonym for **ownership. Good title** means that the buyer takes the goods free from, for example, rights of third parties. Where the seller is the owner, title to the goods will simply pass from him to the buyer. However, the relevant section of the SGA 1979 does not require that the seller is the owner; he merely must have a **right to sell.** A seller who does not himself own the goods can sell them with the permission of the owner and thereby comply with the duty to pass good title. The right to sell must be distinguished from the **power** to transfer title to the goods. 'Power' refers to the ability of the seller to actually transfer property to the buyer. In most cases the two will go together, but there may be situations in which the seller has the right to sell the goods, but not the power to transfer good title, or vice versa.

2. Duty to Deliver

The SGA 1979 requires the seller to **deliver** the goods to the buyer in accordance with the contract. **Delivery** in this context means more than just the dispatch of goods; delivery is the voluntary transfer of **possession** from one person to another. In fact, unless the parties have agreed otherwise, the buyer must collect the goods from the seller's place of business. The seller's duty is limited to ensuring that the buyer can actually do so; he does not have to send the goods anywhere.

Physical transfer of the goods (whether they are sent by the seller or collected by the buyer) is only one of several ways in which delivery can be effected. Delivery may be **symbolic,** if the seller transfers to the buyer the means of controlling the goods, rather than the goods themselves, for example by giving him the keys to the warehouse in which the goods are stored. Where the goods are in the possession of a third party, the seller can instruct that person to hold the goods on behalf of the buyer and no longer for the seller. Delivery takes place when the third party acknowledges that he does indeed now hold the goods for the buyer. This process is called **attornment.** The seller may also transfer to the buyer **documents of title** and thereby effect delivery. The special feature of documents of title is that they represent the goods, and transfer of the document is sufficient to transfer property in the goods. Attornment is not necessary where delivery is by way of transfer of documents of title. Finally the seller can fulfil his obligation to deliver by handing the goods over to an agent of the buyer or the parties may agree that the seller is to retain possession of the goods as the buyer's agent or bailee.

Some contracts contain clauses that free the seller from liability for non-delivery if he can show that he was prevented from performing his obligation. Such clauses are often called **'force majeure'** or **'Act of God'** clauses. 'Force majeure' covers events which make performance impossible for the seller, provided that the event was not reasonably foreseeable and was external, *i.e.* not something the seller was responsible for. Examples include strikes, wars and embargoes. The term 'Act of God', also called ***vis major,*** is very similar to 'force majeure'; the main difference is that *vis major* applies only to natural events, such as floods or earthquakes, not to events which are due to human intervention.

3. Duty to Deliver Goods at the Right Time

A contract of sale can contain various provisions as to **time,** for example as to the time of payment and the time of delivery. The question arises whether such stipulations are **of the essence** of the contract. A term which is of the essence is a condition of that contract, meaning that breach of that term entitles the other party to repudiate the contract and claim damages. Under the SGA 1979 it is a question of construction of the contract whether stipulations as to time of delivery are of the essence, but the courts have decided that in commercial contracts such clauses will normally be conditions. This means that if the seller fails to deliver at the time or during the period set out in the contract, he will be in breach, even if the delay is only a question of hours or even minutes.

Early delivery is as much a breach of contract as **late delivery.** Sometimes the parties allow the seller some degree of flexibility by providing that he is to use **best endeavours** to deliver the goods by a certain date. Alternatively the contract may stipulate for delivery **'as required',** in which case the buyer informs the seller of his requirements and the seller delivers accordingly.

4. Duty to Supply the Right Quantity of Goods

The seller must deliver the correct **quantity,** *i.e.* amount of goods to the buyer. This duty is generally applied very strictly. Any **shortfall** or **excess** entitles the buyer to reject the goods. If the seller delivers a smaller quantity than provided for in the contract he cannot excuse himself by promising to deliver the outstanding amount at a later time, as the buyer does not have to accept delivery by **instalments** unless that is agreed in the contract. In order to give the seller a moderate amount of flexibility the parties often provide for a small margin, for example by setting the amount to be delivered down as '10 tons, 5 percent more or less'.

One exception to the strict application of the duty to deliver the correct quantity is the principle ***'de minimis non lex curat'*** – the law does not concern itself with trifles. According to this rule the buyer cannot reject the goods if the shortfall or excess in question is so small as to be negligible. However, this principle is an exception only and should be treated with care.

5. Duty to Supply Goods of the Right Quality

Under the SGA 1979 a number of terms are implied into contracts of sale to ensure that the seller delivers the correct **quality** of goods. There are several elements in relation to this duty, depending on the contract and the type of goods involved. The terms which are implied and therefore become part of the contract include the following: the goods must correspond with their **description**, the goods must be **fit for the particular purpose** for which they are bought, in a **sale by sample** the bulk must correspond with the sample and the goods must be **satisfactory**. It is not possible to give a straightforward definition of this term, as it depends too much on the kind of goods in question. The SGA 1979 merely lists a number of factors that are to be taken into account in the assessment of the quality of goods, such as the price, their appearance and finish, safety and durability.

IV. Duties of the Buyer

1. Duty to Pay the Price

The buyer must **pay** for the goods in accordance with the terms of the contract of sale. He cannot claim possession until he is ready and willing to pay for them, unless the parties have agreed on a period of credit. In the absence of any stipulation as to the method of payment the buyer has to pay the price in cash, that is money in notes or coins. However, there are a number of other payment mechanisms.

The contract may provide for payment by **cheque** or other negotiable instrument. Such payment is usually treated as **conditional payment** only. The seller is regarded as not having been paid until the cheque has been **honoured** by the bank, *i.e.* he has received the amount specified on the cheque. It should be noted that there is no contractual relationship between the seller and the bank on whom the cheque is drawn. If the cheque is not met the seller can bring an action against the buyer for non-payment, but he has no claim against the bank. This is an important difference between payment by cheque and payment by credit card.

Payment by **credit card** involves a triangle of contracts. First, there is a prior contract between the seller and the credit card company, under which the seller agrees to accept payment by credit card and the company accepts liability for payments made with their cards. Second, there is a prior contract between the buyer and the credit card company. This contract obliges the company to pay for transactions made with their card, while the buyer has to repay the relevant amount to the company. The third contract involved is the contract of sale between seller and buyer, which is the subject of the payment made by credit card. The primary duty to pay is on the credit card company. The seller will approach the company, and not the buyer, for payment. The onus of recovering the money from the buyer is on the company, not the seller.

A more complicated method of payment is **documentary credit**, which is used especially in international transactions. Payment is effected through the banks of each party, rather than being made directly by the buyer to the seller. The basic procedure for opening a **letter of credit** is as follows. Once the parties have agreed on this form of payment the buyer approaches his bank, the **issuing bank**, to open a documentary credit and clarifies which documents, for example the bill of lading, quality certificates etc., are to be provided by the seller. The issuing bank then informs the **correspondent bank**, the bank of the seller, of the fact that a documentary credit has been opened. This information is passed on to the seller who hands the relevant documents over to the correspondent bank. Once the bank is satisfied that the documents comply with the terms of the documentary credit, it pays the purchase price to the seller. The correspondent bank then passes the documents on to the issuing bank, which reimburses the correspondent bank. The issuing bank finally hands the documents over to the buyer in return for payment of the relevant amount. Thus the seller receives the price, while the buyer receives the documents, and through them, the goods.

2. Duty to Accept the Goods

The second obligation of the buyer is the duty to **accept** the goods. He must be ready and willing to **take delivery**, provided that the goods are delivered in the way agreed on in the contract. Failure to collect the goods at the seller's place of business, or refusal to take the goods when they are delivered, amounts to a breach of contract. However, unlike the time of delivery, the time of taking delivery is not normally of the essence.

After the buyer has taken delivery, he is under a further duty to accept the goods, provided that they are in accordance with the contract. In practice this is often perceived as a negative duty, namely the duty not unjustifiably to reject the goods. **Acceptance** is deemed to take place if the buyer informs the seller that he accepts the goods, if he deals with them in a way which is inconsistent with the ownership of the seller (e.g. if the buyer sells them to a third party), or if a reasonable time has elapsed without the buyer indicating his intention to reject the goods.

V. Effects of the Contract

1. Transfer of Property

The main aim of a contract of sale is that **property** in the goods should pass from the seller to the buyer. Property is here used as a synonym for ownership or title. The buyer is to receive the full legal title to the goods and not just a **right of possession**. There are various points at which property might be thought to pass, for example when the contract is formed, when the goods are delivered or when the price is paid. The SGA 1979 has laid down detailed rules in this respect, which focus on whether the goods in question are specific or unascertained goods.

2. Passing of Risk

At any time during the existence of goods there is a danger that they might be accidentally damaged or destroyed. The person who has to bear the cost of any accidental loss is said to be **on risk**. **Risk** is often closely linked with property; usually goods are held **at the**

risk of the owner and under a contract of sale risk often passes to the buyer at the same time as property in the goods passes. However, this does not always have to be so and there may well be situations in which the buyer is on risk even though he is not yet the owner of the goods.

VI. Remedies

1. Remedies of the Seller

The primary obligation of the buyer is payment of the price and if he should fail to do so the seller can bring a **personal action** against him for breach of contract. This action may be a claim for the price of the goods or it may be a claim for damages for non-acceptance. In many cases the personal action against the buyer will be sufficient to compensate the seller for the loss he has suffered. This is not the case, however, if the buyer is insolvent. The seller's claim does not take precedence over the other creditors and he will only receive his proportionate share when the buyer's assets are realised, *i.e.* sold in order to satisfy the creditors. The law has therefore developed a number of so-called **real remedies**, which enable the seller to retain some power over the goods as security for payment, namely the lien, the right of stoppage in transit and the right of re-sale. They apply only if the buyer is insolvent, and in addition the seller must show that he is an **unpaid seller**, which he is if the whole of the price has not been paid or tendered. A seller who has received only some of the money due to him is therefore also regarded as unpaid.

The **unpaid seller's lien** entitles the seller to retain possession of the goods. It should be noted that the lien is the right to retain, not the right to regain possession; it can therefore only be exercised if the seller still has the goods under his control. The seller can keep the goods until the buyer pays the full purchase price.

If the goods are already on their way to the buyer, the seller can use the **right of stoppage in transit** to resume possession. He can stop the transport and again keep possession of the goods until he is paid.

In certain circumstances the seller also has a **right to resell** the goods. The right of **re-sale** must be distinguished from the **power to resell**. The seller has the power to resell the goods if, for example, he is still in possession of the goods even though property has passed to the buyer. If the seller resells the goods in this situation the second buyer will receive good title. However, because the seller does not have a right to resell *vis-à-vis* the original buyer, he will be liable in damages for breach of the first contract of sale. If, on the other hand, the seller has a right of resale he can sell the goods to a second buyer without being in breach of the original contract. The right to resell does not arise automatically as soon as the buyer does not pay. It only arises if, for example, there is an express provision to this effect in the contract or if the goods concerned are perishable.

The so-called real remedies afford the seller a certain amount of protection against non-payment by the buyer. However, they can only be utilised if the seller is still in possession of the goods, or the goods are still in transit. In recent years businessmen have increasingly tried to protect themselves against the possible insolvency of the buyer by retaining title to the goods even after they have been delivered to the buyer. They do so by inserting so-called **retention of title clauses** into the contract of sale. Such clauses stipulate that property in the goods does not pass to the buyer until the full price has been paid, notwithstanding that the goods are delivered before payment is made. Where such clauses are effective the seller remains the owner of the goods, even though he is no longer in possession and he may reclaim the goods on the buyer's insolvency.

2. Remedies of the Buyer

Should the seller fail to deliver any goods at all, the buyer can bring an action against him, claiming damages for non-delivery. If goods are delivered, but it turns out that in some way they do not conform to the contract, the buyer has two possible remedies. He may either claim damages for breach of contract, or he may **reject** the goods, *i.e.* refuse to accept them. If the contract provides for a period in which delivery is to take place, and that period has not yet expired, the seller can **re-tender** delivery within the remaining time. **Rejection** of the goods therefore does not automatically terminate the contract. The contract will be brought to an end, however, if the time for delivery has expired or the defect in the goods is so serious as to amount to a breach of condition. In this case the buyer may reject the goods and **repudiate**, *i.e.* terminate, the contract.

VII. Terminology

Carriage of goods: the law of carriage of goods deals with the transportation of goods by land (by rail or road), air and sea. The movement of goods may take place under a variety of contracts, which are regulated by the law. The law covers the relationship between the parties, implied terms and common exceptions, and specific problems that might arise (for example if a ship deviates from the agreed route).

Choses in action / things in action: the terms can be used synonymously, as can 'chose in possession' and 'thing in possession'.

Collateral contract: a subsidiary contract, consideration for which is the making of a main contract. In the example given, the purchase of goods is the main contract, while the so-called gift is transferred under a collateral contract (and is therefore not a gift at all).

Consumer contract: a contract where one party deals in the course of his business, and the other (the consumer) does not.

Existing / future goods: the terms existing and future goods are not to be applied in the usual way; the important question is not just whether the goods already exist at the time the contract is formed, but whether they are owned or possessed by the seller. Goods that are still owned by a third party when the contract between seller and buyer is formed are future goods for the purposes of that contract.

Goods: includes things such as crops, which are attached to the land, but which are to be severed before completion of the contract of sale.

Negotiable instrument: a document that represents a certain amount of money and has a number of specific characteristics. There are different types of negotiable instruments, which have in common that they exist in order to facilitate commercial transactions.

Option: generally speaking, an option is the right to do or not to do something, *i.e.* the right to chose. In contract law, it denotes the right of one party to accept or refuse an existing offer at a later date. This right is usually contractual and must be bought for valid consideration. In the case of hire-purchase agreements, the buyer can decide at the end of the agreed period, whether he wants to buy the goods or not. The seller has to accept the buyer's decision.

Possession: denotes that someone has physical control over property and intends to use it as his own (whether he is entitled to do so or not). It is often seen as *prima facie* evidence of ownership, but possession and property are distinct legal concepts.

Property: can refer to all things with a monetary value which belong to a person. In this sense property can be divided into **real property** (land; also known as **realty**) and **personal property** (property other than land; also known as **personalty**). Property can furthermore be used as a synonym for 'ownership', which means that a person is entitled to do what he wants with the goods; he can use them, sell them, destroy them and he can exclude other people from interfering with them. Property in this sense must be distinguished from the mere possession of goods. Where the right of ownership is combined with the right of possession a **complete legal title** exists.

Retention of title clauses: also called **reservation of title clauses** or **Romalpa clauses** (after a case in which such a clause was used).

Sale / agreement to sell: there are several synonyms for 'sale' and 'agreement to sell'. The former can also be called **executed sale** or **actual sale**; the latter is an **executory contract of sale** or simply **executory sale**. These terms emphasise the difference between sale and agreement to sell. **Contracts of sale** are also often referred to as **contracts for sale**; these terms are interchangeable and both include sales as well as agreements to sell.

Sale by sample: a contract for the sale of goods under which the seller shows the buyer an example of what the main quantity of the product will look like. It is an implied term of the contract that the bulk which is eventually delivered will have the same characteristics as this sample.

VIII. Review and Discussion

1. *Explain the term 'goods' and distinguish between ownership and possession of goods.*

The first element of the definition is that 'goods' covers only chattels; therefore land cannot be the subject-matter of a contract for the sale of goods. Secondly, only chattels personal are 'goods'; the definition does not include chattels real, which are connected to land. Thirdly, choses in action are excluded from the definition. This refers to certain forms of intangible property, such as copyrights and insurance policies. They can be sold, but their transfer is not covered by the SGA 1979. It can therefore be said that the term 'goods' is defined as tangible property that does not consist of land or an interest in land. Money does comply with this definition, but it is expressly excluded from the definition of 'goods' for the purposes of the SGA 1979.

Ownership means the right to exclusive enjoyment of a thing. The owner of goods can deal with them in whichever way he wants to, and can prevent others from interfering with them. Ownership must be distinguished from possession, which refers to physical control of goods. A person who has actual influence over the goods is in possession, but he is not necessarily the owner. The owner of goods has legal control over them; the possessor only has physical control.

2. *Why is it important to distinguish between contracts of sale and other legal relationships?*

The provisions of the SGA 1979 apply only to contracts for the sale of goods. It is therefore necessary to distinguish between those contracts that do fall within this category and those that do not, because they involve either a sale of something other than goods, or a transfer of goods in some way other than sale. Problems arise if there is an overlap between two kinds of transaction, as when goods are exchanged for both money and other goods. A distinction that can be very difficult to draw in practice is that between contracts of sale and contracts for services, as the latter often include the provision of goods and materials as well as the rendering of a service. Although the law relating to contracts for services is in many respects similar to the SGA 1979, some important differences remain and the distinction must be maintained.

3. *Explain the following: ex works, FAS, FOB, CIF.*

The above are four examples of standard contracts that are often used in commercial (especially international) sales. They set out the duties of each party in relation to the transport and transfer of the goods. The responsibility for making the necessary arrangements can be divided between the parties in different ways, or it may rest solely on either the buyer or the seller.

Under an **ex works** contract the buyer has to arrange for transportation of the goods from the seller's place of business. The seller fulfils his obligation to deliver by allowing the buyer to collect the goods.

FAS stands for **'free alongside ship'**. The seller undertakes to deliver the goods to a ship nominated by the buyer, but he is not obliged to load them. It is for the buyer to arrange for loading and shipment of the goods to their destination.

An **FOB** contract requires the seller to place the goods **'free on board'** the ship nominated by the buyer. This means that he bears the cost of transport to the port and of loading, but not the cost of, for example, insuring the goods.

A **CIF** contract is an agreement to sell goods at an inclusive price, covering the **cost** of the goods, **insurance** and **freight**. The cost of transportation and insurance is borne by the buyer, but it is the responsibility of the seller to make the necessary arrangements.

4. *Until the Sale and Supply of Goods Act 1994 the test for the quality of goods was whether they were 'merchantable'; this was then changed to 'satisfactory'. Which terminology is preferable?*

The first Sale of Goods Act was very much aimed at the merchant community, and requiring goods to be **merchantable** was a logical and meaningful standard to impose. As consumer transactions became more prevalent, however, focus shifted from the simple question whether goods could be sold on, to a more detailed analysis of whether they in fact met the expectations of the buyer. The change introduced by the Sale and Supply of Goods Act 1994 is to be welcomed, because it allows for a much closer monitoring of standards, including minor and cosmetic defects. A new car that has a dent in the side can still be sold (and is therefore merchantable), but it is not satisfactory.

However, the term 'satisfactory' might not be the most appropriate choice. If something is said to be satisfactory, this often implies a relatively low standard, something that is reasonable but not outstanding. The term 'acceptable', which was proposed by the **Law Commission**, a body which makes proposals for law reform, might therefore have been preferable.

Chapter 13: Company Law

I. Introduction

A **company** is one of several forms in which a business enterprise can be organised. Alternatives include the **sole trader** and the **partnership**. The former is simply an individual engaged in business; the latter consists of two or more people working together. Companies also usually involve more than one person, but there are important differences to the partnership. One of the central features of a company is that management is separated from ownership (and often vested in different people). The company structure has important advantages, for example in cases of **insolvency**, and it is consequently one of the most popular forms of business venture. A significant amount of the law relating to companies has been set out in statutes, particularly the **Companies Act 2006**.

II. Birth of a Company

1. Nature of Registered Companies

When a company is formed it is said to be **incorporated**. This can be effected either by a special statute, which creates a **statutory company**, or by **registration** under the Companies Act, which requires the payment of a fee and the delivery of certain documents to the **Registrar of Companies**. Once this procedure has been complied with a **registered company** has been created.

The essential feature of such a company is that it is regarded by law as an independent entity; it is separate from the people who formed it. This entity has a legal status equal to that of a human being, it is an **artificial** or **juristic person**. It can enter into contracts, own property, sue and be sued – all in the name of the company, not that of the individuals involved. However, it cannot act itself (it has a legal, but not a real personality) and relies on human agents, the directors, to conduct its business.

2. Classification of Companies

Every company raises money by allowing people to become members. Most people will become involved in a company in order to make a profit. However, they also undertake a liability towards the company, *i.e.* they have to pay a certain sum of money to it. The amount that a person must contribute, and the time at which he must do so, will depend on the kind of company in question. By far the most important and common type is the **company limited by shares**. The liability of a shareholder to contribute to this company's assets is determined by the amount he has to pay for the shares. Once he has paid for them, he is under no further obligation. A **company limited by guarantee** is similar in that the maximum contribution that may be required is fixed in advance, being a specific amount that a person has agreed to pay. The difference is that here liability only arises if the company is dissolved; nothing has to be paid while the company is a **going concern**. The same is true of **unlimited companies**. However, as the name implies, liability here is not limited to a fixed amount. When the company goes into liquidation every member has to contribute a proportionate amount, regardless of how much that might be.

A further important classification determines how a company can raise capital. A company limited by shares can be organised in the form of either a **public** or a **private com-**

pany. The former is a company which fulfils the statutory requirements (for example in relation to the amount of capital available) and which has been registered accordingly. Every company which is not a public one falls within the residual category of private company. The main advantage of a public company is that it can raise capital by selling shares to the public; private companies, on the other hand, benefit from the fact that they are less tightly regulated.

3. Formalities and Documentation

The key document of any company are its **articles of association**. They govern its operation and will deal with matters such as the issuing and transfer of shares, general meetings, voting rights and the ways in which directors are to conduct the affairs of the company. Together with certain **special resolutions** and agreements the articles form the company's **constitution**. There are statutory rules for the format of articles (for example that they must be contained in a single document), but not for their detailed contents; companies can draft their own, or they can use one of the model articles issued by the Secretary of State. To ensure that people who wish to deal with a particular company can ascertain its main characteristics, the articles must be registered. The articles form a statutory contract between the company and its members, and the members *inter se*.

A further document that is required for the creation of a company is the **memorandum of association**, which sets out the subscribers' intention to establish a company, and to become its members. Once the Registrar is satisfied that all the requirements for registration set out in the Companies Act have been complied with, he will issue a **certificate of incorporation**. This certificate is conclusive evidence that everything is in order and that the company has been registered; it is, in effect, the 'birth certificate' of the registered company.

III. People Involved

1. Promoters

A company cannot form itself, someone must perform the preliminary steps which are necessary for incorporation. A person who intends to, and in fact does, undertake to create a company is known as a **promoter**. The law imposes certain duties on promoters, because they are regarded as being in a fiduciary relationship with the company. One example is that they are not allowed to make a secret profit out of the **promotion**; for example a promoter who sells land to the newly-formed company must disclose the profit he makes from this transaction.

2. Directors

As an artificial legal entity, a registered company relies on agents to conduct its business. These agents are called **directors**, and every company must have at least one (a public company must have at least two). Where there is more than one, company directors act as a **board**. The statutory definition focuses on function, rather than title; people who occupy the relevant position will therefore be regarded as directors, even if they are called, for example, **governors**, **trustees** or the **board of management**.

The Companies Act sets out a list of general duties that are imposed on directors, such as the duty to act within their powers, to promote the success of the company and to exercise reasonable care, skill and diligence. These duties reflect the historical position of directors as fiduciaries. Like all fiduciaries, directors are in a position to affect the company's interests, and the law tries to ensure that this power is not exercised to the company's detriment. For example, a director who wishes to sell a piece of land to the company must disclose his connection with the contract. If he fails to do so, the contract is voidable, because there is a **conflict of interest** between his role as seller and his role as representative of the company. The specific powers, rights and obligations of a director are usually set out in the articles of association; often these will include the power to delegate certain matters to a **managing director** (also often called **chief executive officer – CEO**). What exactly a director does will depend to a large extent on the size of the company in question. In a small company the director will in effect be the manager, responsible for all business decisions. The larger the company the clearer the separation between management and directors will be. Managers will be concerned with the day-to-day running, while directors will lay down corporate policy and deal with the more important decisions. In doing so they must act **bona fide** (in good faith) in the best interests of the company.

3. Secretary

Every company must have a **secretary**. The duties of this position vary significantly, depending on the size of the company and the terms of the individual employment contract. Generally it can be said that the secretary is the administrative officer, responsible for preparing meetings of the board of directors, drafting **minutes** and maintaining accurate registers and records. Usually he can also enter into contracts on behalf of the company, to the extent that this is necessary for administrative purposes.

IV. Membership

The **members** of a company are people who **subscribed** to the memorandum of association and thus became members on incorporation, and any other person whose name is entered on the **register of members**. If a company is limited by shares the term member is synonymous with **shareholder**. A common way of becoming a member is to buy shares from a previous member or on the **stock exchange**.

The main liability of a member of a company limited by shares is to pay for his shares. His rights include the right to vote at meetings (and thereby participate in the running of the company) and the entitlement to receive a **dividend** when it has been declared. The dividend is that part of the company's profits which is divided among the members. Only money which is **declared** as dividend can be paid out, and if no profit is made, or the directors decide not to declare a dividend, the shareholder cannot demand payment.

Membership terminates when the member's name is removed from the register; this happens when, for example, the person in question has transferred all his shares to someone else, or the company itself is dissolved.

V. Shares

1. Introduction

A person who buys a **share** obtains an interest in the company in question. This means that he has certain rights which are legally recognised and enforced. Unfortunately it is not easy to explain the nature of these rights; the concept of the share has always been difficult to define, and there is at present much academic discussion as to whether the rights in question are essentially contractual or proprietary.

Shares can be obtained in different ways. They can, for example, be sold by a member to another person, or they can be issued directly by the company to new members. This process is known as **allotment**. The amount of shares that can be issued by a company is determined by its memorandum of association. This must state the amount of the company's **share capital** (*i.e.* how much money it can raise by selling shares) and into how many shares of a fixed value it is divided.

Shares are a form of intangible property. The physical representation of the share is the **share certificate**. This document is the formal declaration by the company that the shareholder has been registered as a member. It is not a document of title (*i.e.* mere transfer of the document does not transfer ownership of the shares), but it is *prima facie* evidence of the holder's title. The precise form of the share certificate is governed by the articles of incorporation.

2. Types of Shares

There are a number of different types of shares, which give the shareholders different rights in relation to the payment of dividends. The holder of **ordinary shares** has three general rights. He can exercise one vote at general meetings for each share that he holds, he is entitled to the payment of dividend (provided that one has been declared) and if the company is dissolved he will receive a proportionate part of the realised assets. The specific rights relating to ordinary shares are often varied in the memorandum or the articles; a company can, for example, issue two classes of ordinary shares which carry different voting rights.

The rights of owners of **preferential shares** take precedence over ordinary shareholders. These preferential rights may relate to either the dividend, or the return of capital (on dissolution of the company), or both. In relation to dividend, for example, this means that ordinary shareholders will only be paid after all holders of preferential shares have received their money. The risk of profits being insufficient to cover all payments is therefore placed primarily on the owners of ordinary shares. However, these shares also offer an advantage. Both the dividend and proportion of capital payable to preference shareholders is fixed and will therefore not reflect an increase in profit. After the specific amount of preference dividend has been paid, the whole of the remaining profit will be distributed proportionately among the ordinary shareholders.

A third type, **deferred shares**, are now rarely used. The holders of these shares, also called **founders' shares**, are entitled to payment of a dividend only after a fixed rate has been paid to preferential and ordinary shareholders.

VI. Capital

The term **capital** is difficult, if not impossible to define. In a commercial context, the capital of a company is the value of its assets minus the amount it owes to any **creditors**, *i.e.* its net worth. More generally, people might think of capital as referring to the amount of money which was used to start a company and which it now has available to make a profit (the money which has been invested in it). In company law, the term has a much more technical meaning, because there are different types of capital. The **authorised capital**, for example, is the amount which the company can raise by selling shares.

This is specified in the memorandum of association, and might be something like "£50,000 in £1 shares". That part of the authorised capital that has actually been issued to shareholders at a particular time is called **issued** or **allotted capital.** If half of the 50,000 shares have been sold, the company has an issued capital of £25,000.

VII. General Meetings

Many important decisions concerning the company, for example a change to the articles of association by **special resolution**, can only be taken by the shareholders at a **general meeting.** A meeting which is attended by and concerned only with people who hold a particular class of shares is known as a **class meeting**; general meetings involve all members.

A registered company must convene an **annual general meeting (AGM)** once a year. It is called by the directors and will usually deal with a variety of issues: members are informed of the dividend that has been declared, they consider the accounts and balance sheets and might, for example, elect a new director to replace someone who is retiring. Any general meeting of the company which is not an AGM, is an **EGM** – an **extraordinary general meeting.** Generally the calling of an EGM is at the discretion of the directors, but there are circumstances where such a meeting must be called, for example if there is a significant fall in the company's net assets. All general meetings, whether annual or extraordinary, are subject to detailed rules of procedure.

VIII. Shareholder Remedies

As has already been explained, directors have significant powers in relation to the running of a company. This raises the question as to what remedies are available to a shareholder if he feels that a director (or directors) has misconducted himself in some way. Three main types of action can be brought against a director, depending on whether a shareholder believes that his own rights have been infringed, or whether the alleged harm has occurred to the company.

A **personal action** will be appropriate where a personal right of an individual has been infringed. If the right in question is that of a number of shareholders, an individual can bring a **representative action** on behalf of the group.

If a member is of the opinion that the conduct of a director has caused harm to the company itself (as opposed to the individual shareholder), he can bring a **derivative action.** Any benefit gained from this will go to the company, not the member. However, the ability to bring such an action was limited by the important **rule in *Foss v Harbottle*** (reported at (1843) 2 Hare 461), which states that *prima facie* the proper claimant in a case of alleged harm to the company is the company itself, a position based on the recognition of the separate legal personality of the company as a juristic person. Furthermore, an individual cannot bring an action in relation to a matter which, although it is irregular, can be made binding on the company by a simple majority of its members. The underlying idea here is the principle of **majority rule.** There is little point in allowing an action to be brought, if the majority of shareholders can simply ratify the act in question. The common law developed a narrow exception to this rule, meaning that a derivative action was only possible where the shareholder could show that there had been an abuse of power (**'fraud on the minority'**) and that the wrongdoers, *i.e.* the directors, would prevent the company from bringing an action in its own name (**'wrongdoer con-**

trol'). The Companies Act broadens the situations in which derivative actions can be brought, but it remains to be seen how the relevant provisions, which have not been in force long, will be applied by the courts.

A further statutory remedy for aggrieved members allows a shareholder to petition the court for relief if the company's affairs are run in a way which is **unfairly prejudicial** to all or some of the members. Examples of such conduct include abuse of power, mismanagement and **self-dealing** by directors. Self-dealing occurs, for example, if the director sells property to the company at an exaggerated price, the problem being that his duties to the company and his personal interests conflict.

IX. Winding-up

A company is created by registration, and it is terminated, *i.e.* **dissolved** when its name is removed from the register. This usually happens in the form of the **liquidation** of the company, a process also referred to as **winding-up**. This will be necessary if, for example, the company is unable to pay its debts or simply ceases to trade. A **liquidator** will be appointed to **realise** and distribute the **assets** of the company. This means that he will turn everything the company owns into money (for example by selling property) and pay all the creditors the amount that they are owed. If there is a surplus, *i.e.* money remaining after all the creditors have been paid off, it will be distributed among the shareholders.

The winding-up process may be initiated either by the shareholders (**voluntary winding-up**), or by the court following a petition submitted, for example, by a creditor (**compulsory winding-up**). The main advantage of voluntary winding-up is that there are fewer formalities to comply with. Either procedure may be a **solvent** or an **insolvent liquidation**. If the company is solvent when it is wound up, the assets will provide sufficient funds to pay all debts, and the remaining money is paid to the shareholders, who are known as **contributories** when the company is in liquidation. In many cases, however, the company will be unable to pay its creditors, even after all its assets have been realised. The main aim of such an insolvent liquidation is to satisfy the creditors, and contributories will not receive any money (very often even the creditors do not get the whole amount to which they are entitled).

X. Terminology

Board: the directors of a company must generally act as a board, *i.e.* as a group.

Company: in law, 'the company' is a specific entity. In practice, however, this term covers a wide variety of organisations, ranging from small family businesses to international corporations. This reality is recognised to some extent by the Companies Act.

Creditor: someone to whom a debt is owed.

***Foss v Harbottle*:** (1843) 2 Hare 461 is an old law report.

Going concern: a company is a going concern while it is operating as a business. It can thus be distinguished from a company that is in liquidation or has ceased to trade.

Insolvency: the inability of a company or person to pay their debts when they are due.

Limited company: the official abbreviation (recognised by statute) for a limited company is **ltd** (e.g. Smith ltd).

Minutes: notes taken at company meetings, which provide a record of all business transacted.

Partnership: one form in which a business can be organised; it exists when two or more people work together to generate a profit.

Public company: the official abbreviation (recognised by statute) for a public limited company is **plc** (e.g. Smith plc).

Secretary: an important officer of the company, with extensive duties; he should not be confused with a general office secretary, responsible for typing letters and answering telephone calls.

Shareholder: a person who owns shares. In the case of a company limited by shares this term is synonymous with member.

Stock exchange: the organised market for shares and **stocks** (stocks are shares in a company that have been converted into one unit).

XI. Review and Discussion

1. How can companies be classified?

Companies can be classified in many different ways, depending, for example, on their size or the number of employees. One fundamental classification relates to the extent of liability undertaken by members. If the amount of money a member has to contribute is restricted to a fixed amount, the company is a limited company. The contribution may be simply the amount that the member has agreed to pay, in which case the company is one limited by guarantee, or it may be determined by the number of shares he owns. This is the company limited by shares, by far the most important and numerous type. In the case of an unlimited company, the liability of members is not limited to a specific amount; the sum payable is only determined on the liquidation of the company. Unlimited companies and companies limited by guarantee have in common that liability arises only when the company is dissolved; the obligation of a member of a company limited by shares to pay the amount due on his shares can be called in at any time.

Companies limited by shares can be further classified according to the way in which they can raise capital. In order to be able to sell shares to the general public, a company must be registered as a public company. All companies which are not so registered are private companies. Selling shares to the public is an important way of raising capital (especially for large companies), but private companies have the advantage of being less tightly regulated.

2. What are the most important documents for a company?

The memorandum of association is a statement by the subscribers that they intend to set up the company, and to become its members. The memorandum must be submitted to the Registrar together with the articles of association. They are a key document of the company's constitution, and set out how the company is to operate, for example by clarifying the allocation of power between the members and the directors. Articles will usually deal with things like shares, general meetings, voting rights and rules of conduct for the directors, but the details are for each company to decide (as long as the statutory rules as to format are complied with). Instead of drafting their own, companies can also use model articles. Once the relevant documents have been filed with the Registrar and he is satisfied that all elements of the registration process have been observed, he will issue a certificate of incorporation.

3. What are the differences between a company and a partnership?

Both the company and the partnership are important forms of business organisation. However, there are significant differences between them. Perhaps the most crucial one is that the company has a separate legal personality, while a partnership does not. There is therefore no split between ownership and management in partnerships, and all partners are **jointly liable**. This means that they have to use their personal fortune to pay for debts, including debts incurred by another partner. Members of a company are not personally liable, because any debt belongs to the company itself. Further, there are far fewer formalities for the creation of a partnership than the registration of a company, and, unlike partnerships, companies have to pay **corporation tax**.

The **limited liability partnership** is a hybrid between a company and a partnership. It must be registered and limits the liability of members to the money they have invested, but retains many of the other features of a partnership.

4. Explain the following terms: proxy, prospectus, debenture.

If a member of a company is unable or unwilling to exercise his voting rights in person, he can appoint someone as a so-called **proxy**, to do so on his behalf.

A **prospectus** is the document used to offer shares to the public. It will contain relevant information on the company and the shares in question. Strictly speaking the prospectus is only an invitation to treat, the offer to enter into a contract is made by the prospective purchaser.

A **debenture** is the document by which a company acknowledges the debt it owes to a creditor. It sets out the details of the loan, relating to, for example, repayment and payment of interest. The debenture differs from a share in that the holder is a creditor, not a member of the company. For the sake of convenience borrowed money can be consolidated into one mass, which is then known as **debenture stock**.

Chapter 14: European Union Law

I. The European Communities

Most people think of "the EC" as a single entity. In fact there were initially three Communities, the **European Coal and Steel Community** (ECSC – this no longer exists), the **European Atomic Energy Community** (**Euratom**) and the **European Community** (**EC**). All three organisations share (or shared) the same institutions, but their laws and procedures differ (for example in relation to the legislative process). The EC is by far the most important of the three, and the ECSC and Euratom will not be considered separately.

The EC was founded as the **European Economic Community** (**EEC**) in 1957, when Belgium, France, Germany, Italy, Luxembourg and the Netherlands signed the **Treaty of Rome** (also known as the **EC Treaty**). The United Kingdom joined on 1 January 1973 by signing an **accession treaty** and giving force to EC law within its national legal system by passing the **European Communities Act 1972.** Other countries followed, with the most recent expansion taking place in 2007. Currently there are 27 **Member States:** Austria, Belgium, Bulgaria, Cyprus, the Czech Republic, Denmark, Estonia, Finland, France, Germany, Greece, Hungary, Ireland, Italy, Latvia, Lithuania, Luxembourg, Malta, the Netherlands, Poland, Portugal, Romania, Slovakia, Slovenia, Spain, Sweden and the United Kingdom.

It is important (but perhaps not always easy) to distinguish the European Community from the **European Union** (**EU**). The EU is a separate entity, created by the **Treaty on European Union** (**TEU**), also known as the **Maastricht Agreement,** which came into force in 1993. The EU is composed of three 'pillars', with the EC being the first one. Following amendments introduced by the **Treaty of Amsterdam** (**ToA**) in 1997 the second and third pillars are the **Common Foreign and Security Policy** (**CFSP**) and **Police and Judicial Co-operation in Criminal Matters** (**PJCC**) respectively.

A further brief comment on the ToA is required at this point. The continued process of amendment of the Treaties led to some complications regarding the numbering of Articles. The ToA has sought to remedy this by renumbering all the provisions of the EC Treaty and the TEU. This will necessarily lead to some confusion, as older cases and books still refer to the old numbers. In the following, both numbers will always be given.

Since 1997 the Member States have continued to push ahead with proposals for a more cohesive Europe. The **Treaty of Nice** (**ToN**) was adopted in 2000 to deal with issues raised by enlargement. Following the rejection of the Treaty establishing a **Constitution for Europe** by French and Dutch voters in 2005, the Member States signed the new **Treaty of Lisbon** (also known as the **Reform Treaty**) in 2007. Unlike the Constitution, this is intended to amend, rather than replace, the EC Treaty and the TEU. Following a second referendum in Ireland in October 2009, the Lisbon Treaty will enter into effect as soon as it is formally ratified by all Member States. The EC Treaty will then be renamed **Treaty on the Functioning of the European Union** (**TFEU**). The current three pillar structure will be abolished; the EU will replace the EC and gain legal personality.

II. The Political Institutions of the EC

1. The Commission

There are 27 **commissioners**, one from each Member State. They are nominated by their national governments and must be approved by the European Parliament. The commissioners are not representatives of their country but are expected to act independently and not to follow instructions from their government. The **Commission**, which is located in Brussels, is perhaps the most 'European' of the institutions. Nevertheless, it does take account of the interests of Member States. It is also responsible to the European Parliament and can be censured by it.

The Commission combines a number of different functions which are administrative, legislative and executive in nature. Its main powers include the right to propose legislation, something which allows the Commission significantly to influence policy. It is also responsible for overseeing the implementation of such policies and can take a Member State to court for infringements of EC law. Finally, it plays an important part in relation to the **budget**.

The Lisbon Treaty provides for a reduction of the size of the Commission from 27 to a number corresponding to two thirds of the Member States. Participation will rotate between the countries. This change will come into effect in 2014. If there are still 27 Member States at that point, the new number of commissioners will therefore be 18.

2. The Council

The full name of this body is the **Council of the European Union**. It usually convenes in Brussels, although some meetings take place in Luxembourg. The **Council**, as it is usually referred to, has 27 members, one from each Member State. Its composition is not fixed; the national governments send representatives in accordance with the subject-matter in question. Thus a meeting on agriculture will be attended by, for example, the agriculture ministers, a meeting on employment by employment ministers. Unlike the commissioners, members of the Council are there as representatives of their country and can commit their national governments.

The Council votes on legislative proposals submitted by the Commission, it represents the EC in relation to third countries and decides on the budget. It can also delegate powers to the Commission. However, the Council is normally limited to Commission proposals and in an increasing number of circumstances it must work with the Parliament before being able to adopt a legislative measure.

Most decisions are taken by a **qualified majority vote**, using a weighted voting system. Under the Lisbon Treaty, this will become a **double majority**, with decisions requiring the assent of 55 percent of Member States representing at least 65 percent of the population.

The members of the Council receive important assistance from the **Committee of Permanent Representatives of the Member States**, usually known by its French acronym **COREPER**. This permanent body prepares much of the Council's work, thereby providing the continuity which that body lacks because of its fluctuating membership.

The Council should not be confused with the **European Council**. This body, which was given legal recognition by the **Single European Act** (**SEA**) of 1986, comprises the Heads of State or Government of all Member States. Its ambit is to define the general political guidelines of the EU and to provide it with the impetus necessary for its development. The Treaty of Lisbon grants the European Council the status of an official European **institution.**

3. The European Parliament

The 736 **Members of the European Parliament (MEPs)** are directly elected by the citizens of the Member States every five years. The number of MEPs from each Member State depends on the size of its population; once elected they sit in groups representing political affiliation, not in national blocks. The **European Parliament** is located in Strasbourg, but some sessions take place in Brussels, and most of its support staff are placed in Luxembourg.

Initially the European Parliament operated mainly as an advisory body, but over time its powers have increased significantly. It plays an important role in the legislative process, together with the Council it controls the budget, it must approve the Commissioners nominated by the Member States and it can dismiss the Commission by passing a **vote of censure.** In some circumstances, such as the admission of new Member States, it even has a right of veto.

The Lisbon Treaty sets the number of MEPs at 751.

4. The Economic and Social Committee and the Committee of the Regions

The **Economic and Social Committee (ECOSOC)** represents the interests of a variety of people, such as producers, workers, farmers and the general public. Its functions are purely advisory, although in some circumstances consultation of this body is compulsory.

The **Committee of the Regions** was established to advise the Council and the Commission on the interests of regional and local bodies within the Community.

5. The Court of Auditors

The **Court of Auditors** was established in 1975 and obtained the status of an institution of the Community under the TEU. Despite its name, it does not have a judicial function, but controls and supervises the financial management of the EC. It consists of 27 members who must be qualified for this office and whose independence must be beyond doubt.

III. The Legislative Process

EC law provides for no less than three different legislative procedures, each requiring a different level of involvement by the Parliament. Which procedure is applicable in a particular case depends on the Treaty provision which provides the legal basis for the measure in question. It is not possible in this context to describe the complicated legislative process in detail; the following will provide an overview of the key features only.

1. The Consultation Procedure

The influence of the Parliament is at its weakest under the **consultation procedure.** It has the right to be **consulted** by the Council, but its opinion is not in any way binding. The legislative process begins when the Commission submits a proposal to the Council. The draft is then sent to the Parliament, which gives its opinion and can suggest amendments.

The Council can take account of the Parliament's comments, but does not have to do so; it does not even have to give reasons for rejecting them.

2. The Co-operation Procedure

The **co-operation procedure**, introduced by the SEA, initially corresponds with the consultation procedure. However, instead of simply adopting the measure in question, the Council adopts a **'common position'**, which is then sent to the Parliament to be accepted, rejected or amended. If the Parliament approves the common position, or fails to act within a certain time limit, the measure will be adopted by the Council without further changes. If the Parliament rejects the common position, the measure can still be adopted by the Council, but to do so it must act unanimously. Any amendments suggested by the Parliament are considered by the Commission, which decides whether to include them in the proposal or not. The Council can then approve the final proposal with a qualified majority, or amend it by a unanimous vote. The result of all this is that the Council can still ignore the opinion of the Parliament, but must do so unanimously.

3. The Co-decision Procedure

The most complicated process, the **co-decision procedure**, was introduced by the TEU. The procedure is the same as under the co-operation procedure, up to the point at which the Parliament considers the common position. If it approves the common position, or fails to act before the deadline, the process remains the same. However, things change if the Parliament rejects the common position. The Council can convene a **Conciliation Committee**, consisting of an equal number of members from both sides. If this body cannot achieve a result and the Parliament continues to reject the common position, the act is deemed not to have been adopted.

As always the Parliament has the right to propose amendments to the common position. If these suggestions are accepted by the Council, the measure is adopted. If the Council does not approve the amendments, the Conciliation Committee is convened in a further attempt to reconcile the two sides. The Committee will try to agree a **joint text**, to be resubmitted to the Council and the Parliament. If either body fails to approve the joint text, or if the Committee cannot agree on such a text, the measure is rejected. The distinguishing feature of the co-decision procedure is that the Council cannot overrule Parliament's rejection of a proposal.

The co-decision procedure has been increasingly relied on since the ToA and was made more efficient by the ToN, as decisions of the Council are now taken by qualified majority, rather than unanimously. Under the Lisbon Treaty it will be renamed the **ordinary legislative procedure** and its application will be further extended.

IV. The Judicial Institutions of the EC

1. The European Court of Justice

The **European Court of Justice** (ECJ) in Luxembourg is the highest authority on all matters of EC law. Its task is to ensure that EC law is observed and that it is interpreted and applied uniformly. It hears cases brought against Member States for alleged infringements of EC law, and has jurisdiction to resolve disputes between different Community institutions. The ECJ can also review the legality of acts of the institutions and receives preliminary references from national courts and tribunals.

The ECJ consists of 27 judges, who hear cases either as a **Full Court**, as a **Grand Chamber** of 13, or in smaller **Chambers** of three or five judges. Decisions are taken by a majority, but they are always presented as a single judgment of the court. Dissenting or concurring opinions are not reported, a measure which protects the judges from being pressured by national governments.

The judges are assisted by eight **Advocates General**, a position which has no equivalent in the English legal system. The Advocate General assigned to a case prepares a written **opinion**, setting out his analysis of the relevant law and recommending a decision. This document is presented to the ECJ before the judges make their decision. It is intended as impartial and independent advice, and is therefore not binding on the Court. However, it is always considered with great care and is in fact very often followed. The Advocate General's opinion is included in the case report, and can often serve to illustrate points in the judgment.

There is no appeal from judgments of the ECJ. As regards its own earlier decisions, the Court does seek to maintain consistency, but there is no system of binding precedent.

The Lisbon Treaty renames the ECJ the **Court of Justice of the European Union.**

2. The Court of First Instance

The **Court of First Instance** (**CFI**), which is also located in Luxembourg, was established in 1988 to lessen the workload of the ECJ and consists of 27 judges. Cases are heard in Chambers of three or five judges. The jurisdiction of the CIF covers all cases brought by **'non-privileged' parties**, *i.e.* parties other than Community institutions and Member States. Most cases concern applications for judicial review, competition cases and staff cases, that is actions brought against the EC by its employees. Decisions of the CFI can be appealed to the ECJ on points of law.

The Treaty of Nice provides for **judicial panels** to be attached to the CFI to deal with particular types of cases at first instance. A **Civil Service Tribunal** with seven judges has been set up under these provisions; it hears disputes between the European institutions and their employees.

Under the Lisbon Treaty, the CFI is renamed the **General Court** and the judicial panels are renamed **specialised courts.**

V. EC Law

1. Sources of EC Law

The body of law commonly referred to as EC law comes from a variety of sources. The **constitutive Treaties** of the European Communities, and the Treaties that amended them, have already been mentioned. Agreements concluded by the EC with **non-Member States**, such as the establishment of the **World Trade Organisation** (**WTO**), are also significant. The most substantive sources, however, (certainly as regards volume) are Community legislation, the case law developed by the ECJ and general principles of Community law, as developed by the court.

2. Community Legislation

The EC Treaty provides for five different categories of official acts. **Recommendations** and **opinions** are not binding and will not be considered further; they do, however, have persuasive authority.

Regulations lay down general normative rules which must be followed by all Member States. They are **binding in their entirety**. Member States must do exactly what it says in the regulation; they cannot, for example, try to achieve the same result in a way different from that prescribed in the act. All regulations are **directly applicable**, *i.e.* they do not have to be **implemented** by the Member States in order to take effect. As soon as a regulation comes into force, it is automatically part of the law of each Member State.

Directives lay down a particular objective that is to be achieved by the Member States to which they are addressed. It is up to the national authorities to decide on the methods they will use to obtain the required results. All directives must be implemented in order to be effective; they are not directly applicable. This means that the Member States have to **transpose** each directive into national law, for example by passing a statute to that effect. There will normally be a deadline for **implementation**, and failure to comply with it can result in the Commission bringing legal proceedings against the defaulting Member State.

Decisions, like directives, are binding on the addressee. The difference is that directives are always aimed at Member State, while decisions can also be addressed to, for example, individuals and companies in a particular Member State. They are therefore used to deal with individual cases.

3. General Principles of Law

The ECJ often bases its decisions on **general principles of law**; standards which are not expressly contained in the Treaties or any other form of EC legislation, but which nevertheless are of significant import. Some, like the protection of human rights, have been taken from the legal systems of Member States, others can be traced back to the Treaties. The Treaty provision which prohibits discrimination on grounds of nationality, for example, has been extended into a general principle of equality, which proscribes arbitrary **discrimination** on any ground. The following are a few examples of general principles of law that have been recognised and enforced by the ECJ.

One of the key concepts of EC law is **legal certainty**. This principle is not easy to explain in a few words, because it has several applications, but the underlying idea is that the law must be predictable. One important aspect is the protection of **legitimate expectations**. People are entitled to have certain expectations regarding matters affecting their affairs. For example, if a person knows that a particular activity involves a certain charge, it might be reasonable for him to believe that he will have to pay the same amount, if he undertakes the activity in question. If this belief is recognised as a legitimate expectation, it will be protected by EC law. This protection is not absolute, as legitimate expectations can be ignored if there is an overriding public interest in change (and of course an expectation will not be reasonable, if it is known that a change in the law will be introduced in the future), but it does provide an important degree of certainty.

A second application of the principle of legal certainty concerns **retroactivity**. A measure is **retroactive** if it affects something which happened before it came into effect. This will be the case if it changes the law in relation to transactions which were completed before it was valid, or if the transactions concerned are still in the process of being completed. It can obviously cause great hardship to individuals, if, for example, a charge that they paid is simply increased later; all forms of retroactivity are therefore prohibited, unless it can be shown that the objective of the measure could not be achieved in any other way.

The principle of **proportionality** was introduced into the EC Treaty by the TEU. It was developed, however, by the ECJ as an unwritten rule of law. This concept requires that all Community action must be **proportionate** to the objective that is to be achieved. A measure which provides only a small benefit to the public, but causes significant detriment to some individuals, is **disproportionate.** Any authority must try to find a balance between public interest and individual detriment, and must always limit its actions to that which is necessary to bring about a certain result.

Fundamental human rights have acquired a significant status within EC law over the last few years. In this area the national law of Member States is particularly influential, as are international treaties such as the **European Convention for the Protection of Human Rights and Fundamental Freedoms.**

The **Charter of Fundamental Rights of the European Union**, signed in 2000, will take effect under the Lisbon Treaty.

VI. The EC and the Member States

1. Introduction

The EC is a complex organisation, comprising an ever increasing number of Member States with different legal, political and cultural backgrounds. This structure can only operate if the relationship between the EC and its Member States, and between individual Member States, is clearly defined. In order for the EC to be able to function effectively, its law must be applied uniformly, and it must prevail over conflicting national legislation. The United Kingdom recognised the supremacy of EC law in s. 2 of the European Communities Act 1972.

2. Direct Effect

In order to be effective, EC law must be enforceable. The Community can itself act against any Member State that does not fulfil its obligations. The other important enforcement mechanism relies on private individuals and the national courts.

Certain provisions of EC law are capable of having **direct effect.** This means that they grant rights to individuals which must be recognised and enforced by national courts.

The terms direct effect and **direct applicability** are sometimes used interchangeably. However, in order to avoid confusion, a clear distinction will be maintained here. A provision is directly applicable if it automatically becomes part of the legal system of each Member State, without the need for implementation; it is directly effective if it confers rights on individuals which can be enforced before the national courts.

In order to be **directly effective** the provision in question must be sufficiently clear, precise and unconditional. This will not be the case if it is dependent on further action by the authorities, or if it provides for any discretion. Treaty provisions, regulations, directives and decisions have all been held capable of direct effect, although any time limit for the implementation of a directive must have expired, before an individual can directly rely on rights contained in it.

It is clear that there are circumstances where an individual can enforce rights granted by EC law in the national courts. The remaining question is against whom these rights can be enforced. It has been held by the ECJ that directives are capable only of **vertical direct effect**. This means that they can be enforced against the State, but not against private entities or individuals. Thus they confer rights that can be enforced by individuals, but do not impose obligations that can be enforced against individuals. Treaty provisions and regulations, on the other hand, can have both vertical and **horizontal direct effect**; they can be enforced against both the State and individuals.

3. Article 234 References (formerly Article 177 References)

It has already been pointed out that uniform application of the law is vital for the efficient operation of the EC, and it is the task of the ECJ to protect and enforce it. However, questions relating to EC law often arise in cases before national courts. Article 234 (formerly 177) provides a mechanism for such issues to be **referred** to the ECJ for a **preliminary ruling**, a procedure known as an **Article 234 reference** (formerly **Article 177 reference**).

The national court refers only those issues which relate to EC law, for example concerning the interpretation of a Treaty provision, or the validity of a particular piece of legislation. The ECJ will not look at issues of fact or national law and it does not decide the case itself. Once the ECJ has made its preliminary ruling, the case is sent back to the national court which applies the ECJ decision to the facts and decides the case.

Article 234 (formerly 177) distinguishes between courts which *can* make a reference to the ECJ, and courts which *must* do so. The decisive factor is whether any judicial remedies are available to the parties against the decision of the court in question. If the case can go to appeal, reference to the ECJ is **discretionary**; if no appeal is possible (for example if the case in question is before the Supreme Court – fomerly the House of Lords), the reference is **obligatory**. Tribunals other than courts can also refer questions to the ECJ, provided that they are judicial, rather than for example administrative, bodies.

VII. Substantive EC law

It is not possible in this context to give a complete overview of substantive EC law, but the following will provide a brief illustration of some of the main principles. All have a strong commercial element, which reflects the fact that the EC began its life as the European Economic Community. One of its central aims has been the creation of the **internal market**, a territory with no internal boundaries as regards the free movement of goods, persons, services and capital.

1. Free Movement of Goods

Under the rules relating to the **free movement of goods**, dealing with goods within the EC is intended to be like dealing with them within an individual Member State. To ensure that goods can move between Member States without restrictions, **customs duties** and **charges having equivalent effect** have been abolished, as have **quantitative restrictions** on imports and exports and **measures having equivalent effect**. Customs duties and charges having equivalent effect can never be justified; quantitative restrictions and measures having equivalent effect are only permissible if they can be justified on grounds such as public policy, public health, or the protection of national treasures.

2. Free Movement of Workers

The right to move without restriction within the EC has been granted not only to goods, but also to workers; people generally have the right to work in other Member States under the provisions on the **free movement of workers**. A worker who takes advantage of these rights is known as a **migrant worker**. A person may go to another Member State to look for work, and he is entitled to stay there as long as, and even after, he is employed. Employers are not allowed to discriminate against nationals of other Member States in relation to, for example, pay and terms of employment. The exception is employment in the public service, which can be restricted to people who are nationals of the country in question. The free movement of persons can be limited on grounds of public policy, public security and public health.

3. Freedom of Establishment and Free Movement of Services

Free movement rights also extend to the **self-employed** and those wishing to provide or receive **services** in another Member State. **Freedom of establishment** and **free movement of services** are often dealt with together, because the provisions are very similar. Generally it can be said that establishment in a **host state** in order to carry on a business there is of a more permanent nature, while the provision of services is usually temporary. The former entitles the person in question to a right of permanent residence, while the latter entitles a person to stay in a Member State for as long as the service is provided. Both concepts apply to natural and legal persons, and are subject to some restrictions on the basis of public policy, security and health.

4. Free Movement of Capital

The final aspect of the free movement provisions relates to the **free movement of capital**. Significant changes have been introduced which are aimed at ensuring that all persons resident in one Member State can transfer capital to another Member State, and even, to a more limited degree, to non-Member States, without restrictions. Thus it has become easier, for example, to open a bank account in another country. This freedom is not unlimited, however, as individual Member States can impose restrictions based on public policy and public security.

The harmonisation of the capital market is an important part of the development of the internal market. As such it must be seen in conjunction with an area which can perhaps be described as one of the most important (and controversial) developments within the EU: **Economic and Monetary Union** (**EMU**). The economic policy of the Community has progressed in stages; the first two were aimed at harmonising Member States' economies in order to prepare them for the final stage, the introduction of a single currency. The **euro** was introduced on 1 January 1999 in 11 Member States who were found to have complied with the **convergence criteria** – economic targets relating to, *inter alia* rates of inflation and budget deficits. Greece and Sweden had failed to meet those targets, while Denmark and the United Kingdom opted out of the so-called **eurozone**. Responsibility for the operation of the new currency was given to the **European Central Bank** (**ECB**), which started to issue bank notes and coins on 1 January 2002; these replaced national currencies by 1 July of the same year. Other Member States joined once they met the convergence criteria, and the eurozone currently has 16 members.

VIII. Terminology

Article 234 reference: there are two important differences between a reference, such as the Article 234 (formerly 177) reference, and an appeal. First, an appeal is brought by one of the parties, while in the case of a reference the national court decides whether a question should be referred. Secondly, an appeal court decides the entire case; the decision of the lower court is eclipsed by the judgment of the higher court. A reference relates only to specific questions, and the ECJ will only look at the issues that have been referred. The case itself is decided by the national court, which can decide how the ruling of the ECJ should be applied to the facts.

Budget: the expected sum of the Community's income and expenditure for a year.

Charges having equivalent effect: a charge that is levied on goods because they cross a border can produce the same result as a customs duty (*i.e.* making the goods more expensive), even if it does not technically qualify as one. Such charges are known as 'charges having equivalent effect' to customs duties.

Constitutive Treaties: those that created the three communities, *i.e.* the EEC Treaty (the Treaty of Rome), the ECSC Treaty and the Euratom Treaty.

Council: also called the **Council of Ministers.**

Customs duties: charges that have to be paid on certain goods when they are imported into or exported from a particular country.

Direct effect: a measure of EC law is directly effective if it grants rights to individuals that can be enforced in the national courts. This must not be confused with direct applicability.

Directly applicable: a measure of EC law is directly applicable, if it automatically becomes part of the national law of each Member State, without the need for separate enactment. This must not be confused with direct effect.

Discrimination: the principle of discrimination as applied in EC law comprises two elements, namely a difference in the treatment of persons who are in similar situations, and the absence of an objective justification for this dissimilar treatment.

European Convention for the Protection of Human Rights and Fundamental Freedoms: in 1950 the **Council of Europe** (an organisation for co-operation in Europe) drafted the European Convention for the Protection of Human Rights and Fundamental Freedoms (usually called the European Convention on Human Rights). This convention is aimed at protecting fundamental rights, such as the right to life, to freedom from torture and slavery, and to a fair trial. The Council of Europe should not be confused with the European Council; some of the members of the Council of Europe are not Member States of the European Union.

European Court of Justice: must not to be confused with the **European Court of Human Rights,** set up under the European Convention on Human Rights.

European Parliament: initially called the **Assembly.**

Full Court: also called a **plenary session.**

Implement: a Member State implements EC law by passing national legislation to make EC law part of its internal law.

Institution: the EU currently has five official institutions, namely the Council, the Parliament, the Commission, the Court of Auditors and the European Court of Justice. The Lisbon Treaty adds the European Council and the European Central Bank.

Internal market: also referred to as the **single market.**

Legal certainty: also sometimes referred to as **legal security.**

Quantitative restrictions: a **quota,** *i.e.* a limit placed on the amount of goods that can be imported or exported.

Regulation: in EC law, the term 'regulation' refers to one type of Community legislation (to be distinguished from, for example, directives). In English law, however, it can also refer to a form of delegated legislation (to be distinguished from, for example, statutory instruments). This can be especially confusing when (delegated legislation) regulations are used to implement EC law. Thus the EC **Directive on Unfair Terms in Consumer Contracts** was incorporated into English law by the **Unfair Terms in Consumer Contracts Regulations.**

Self-employed: a person who carries out a business on his own account, *i.e.* who does not work for someone else under a contract of employment. In practice the distinction can be difficult to draw.

Services: it is not always easy to distinguish the provision of services from the sale of goods. Generally it can be said that freedom of service covers those services (usually provided in return for some form of payment) that do not fall under the provisions relating to the movement of capital, goods or persons.

WTO: an international trade organisation aimed at promoting free world trade. It replaced the **General Agreement on Tariffs and Trade (GATT)** and lays down trading rules which are very important in the international market.

IX. Review and Discussion

1. ***How does the balance of power between the three institutions differ in relation to the different legislative procedures?***

The Commission is the body responsible for proposing legislation. It therefore has a significant influence on the development of EC law, regardless of which legislative procedure is used. The distribution of power between the Council and the Parliament, however, depends on the type of legislative process. Under the consultation procedure the Council must consult the Parliament, *i.e.* it must give the Parliament the opportunity to state its opinion and propose amendments. However, it is in no way obliged to pay any attention to what the Parliament says, and can adopt the measure by a majority vote. The co-operation procedure places the Parliament in a more influential position. The Council can still ignore the Parliament's opinion, but only if it acts unanimously (something which in practice is not easy to achieve). Under the co-decision procedure, however, the Parliament can prevent a proposal from becoming law; the Council cannot overrule a rejection by the Parliament (not even by a unanimous vote). The Parliament is the only Community institution that is directly elected by the citizens of the Member States: the strengthening of its powers therefore reflects an important shift in the focus of the EC.

2. ***What are the differences between regulations and directives?***

Both directives and regulations are forms of Community legislation, but they differ in their content and effect. Regulations are binding in their entirety. The Member States have no discretion, they must follow the wording of the regulation to the letter. Directives, on the other hand, only lay down a particular objective. How this aim is to be achieved is left to the Member States; they can thus chose the means that are most suited to their circumstances.

A further important difference is that regulations are directly applicable, while directives are not. A regulation automatically becomes part of the national law of each Member State, as soon as it enters into force. Directives must be implemented, *i.e.* each Member State must actively make it part of its national law. One way in which this can be done is by an act of Parliament, which states that the directive in question is to be legally valid. Every directive will set out a time limit by which it must be implemented; a Member State that fails to comply with this deadline is in breach of its obligations and may be held responsible.

3. ***How can EC law be enforced against a Member State?***

The Commission has the power to initiate proceedings against any Member State it considers to be in breach of its obligations. If the ECJ concludes that the charges are justified, for example because the Member State has failed to implement a directive or to comply with a ruling of the Court, it will issue a declaration to this effect. This remedy, which has at times proved ineffective, has now been supplemented by the power of the ECJ to impose a fine on any Member State that does not comply with the declaration. Legal action can also be brought by one Member State against another (although most cases are initiated by the Commission).

Individuals can also enforce EC law against the State, provided that the measure in question is directly effective. A person who can show that he has suffered damage as a result of the Member State's breach of EC law, can also claim damages under the **Francovich principle** of state liability (so named after the case in which it was established).

4. ***Explain the terms 'indirect effect' and 'acte clair doctrine'.***

The ECJ has tried on several occasions to ensure the effective enforcement of EC directives, even where they are not capable of direct effect. It has therefore established the doctrine of **indirect effect**. This requires Member States to interpret national law in the light of directives, irrespective of whether the legislation in question predates the directive or not.

National courts have on occasion refused to refer a particular question of EC law to the ECJ, claiming that the answer is so clear that no preliminary ruling is required. The ECJ has accepted that this can be permissible under the so-called acte clair **doctrine**, if the national court is not only convinced that the answer is clear, but feels certain that the courts in other Member States and the ECJ would agree. However, although the ECJ has recognised the existence of the doctrine, it remains clear that in principle issues of EC law should be referred by national courts.

Chapter 15: Other Areas of Law

I. Classifications of Law

Law can be classified in a number of ways. The differences between common law and equity, and between case law and statute have already been dealt with in other chapters. There are, however, several other divisions. One is the distinction between national law, *i.e.* the domestic law of the country, and **international law**. International law, also known as the **law of nations** or ***jus gentium***, regulates the relationship between sovereign states. It therefore deals with matters such as boundaries, human rights, international crimes and the law of sea and space. This body of rules is also referred to as **public international law**, in order to distinguish it from **private international law**. Despite its name, private international law is part of English law, namely that part which lays down rules for cases containing a foreign element. Thus, for example, if a contract is formed between two companies from different countries, it will be necessary to decide which system of law governs the agreement. The answer to that question, and to issues such as whether an English court has jurisdiction over a particular case involving more than one country, can be found in private international law (or **conflict of laws**, as it is also known).

National law can be further divided into **public law** and **private law**. The former comprises areas such as constitutional, administrative and criminal law, *i.e.* areas that regulate the relationship between individuals and the state (or between one state and another). Public law rules determine, for example, what a public authority can do, and what rights and duties (such as payment of taxes) a person has *vis-à-vis* the state. Private law, on the other hand, deals with relationships between individuals which do not directly concern the state. Such rights and obligations arise, for example, from contract law, tort and company law.

Finally, everything that is not criminal law, is classified as **civil law**.

II. Other Areas of Law

The following is intended to provide a short overview of other areas of law that have not been dealt with specifically. The list is not intended to be authoritative or exhaustive, as many areas of law can be organised in different ways. Insurance law, for example, can be regarded as part of the law of contract, but is usually dealt with separately. It is also possible to bring together under one heading different areas of law which relate to a particular problem or activity. An example of this is **construction law**, which includes things like contract law, tort, insolvency and health and safety law, as they apply to the construction industry. Finally, as social and technological advances raise new issues, new areas of law come to be recognised, such as **media law** and **human rights law**.

Administrative law governs the rights, powers and duties of public bodies, such as ministers of the Crown and local authorities. If an individual feels that his rights have been infringed, for example because the correct procedure was not followed, he can challenge the decision in question before the courts. This process, called **judicial review**, enables the courts to control executive functions.

Banking law is a mixture of contract law, the law of agency and special rules of banking procedure, aimed at regulating the relationship between banks and their customers (and between different banks). It lays down rules for all the different services provided, such as deposit-taking, loans and financial advice, and imposes a number of duties on banks, such as the **duty of confidentiality**.

Criminal law deals with the rules on criminal behaviour, its definition, effect and punishment. It is not easy to define the term 'crime' because it covers a multitude of acts (or omissions), ranging from minor traffic offences to **murder**. Generally it can be said to cover behaviour which is regarded as so morally reprehensible, destructive or disruptive that it requires sanctioning by the state through the medium of criminal trial and conviction. The two main forms of punishment are imprisonment and fines.

Employment law covers all aspects of the employment relationship, including the formation, content and termination of the contract of employment, employees' rights (such as equal pay and **maternity rights**) and health and safety. It is also referred to as **industrial law** or **labour law**. This 'individual' employment law can be distinguished from **trade union law** or **labour relations law**, which deals with the collective elements of employment, namely the internal and external workings of trade unions.

Environmental law initially consisted of those aspects of law that dealt with issues relating to the **environment**. It is now recognised as a separate subject, but retains its close link with areas such as tort (through, for example, nuisance and the rule in *Rylands v Fletcher*) and property law. It deals with the protection of air, water and land, by, *inter alia*, regulating pollution, water quality and waste management, and by promoting nature conservation.

Family law regulates the legal aspects concerning the institution of the family. This generally refers to people who are related by blood, marriage or adoption, although for some purposes other people, such as unmarried partners, can also be included. The main focal points of family law are the concept of marriage and children; thus it deals with questions relating to the legal effects of marriage, the distribution of property in the case of divorce, and the care and adoption of **minors**.

Insurance law centres around the contract of **insurance**, and is thus subject to the general rules of contract law. There are, however, a significant number of principles which are specific to the insurance relationship, such as the **duty of disclosure**. The law controls the formation and contents of the insurance contract, the payment of **premiums** and the making of claims. In addition, there are special rules relating to specific types of insurance, such as life insurance, motor insurance and fire insurance.

Intellectual property law deals with the protection of non-tangible property rights, that is rights relating to ideas and concepts rather than land or goods. The law defines what sort of rights can be protected in this way, the extent of this protection, and how it can be enforced. Intellectual property rights include **patents, copyrights** and **trade marks**.

Land law is concerned with the rights and obligations which can exist in relation to **land**. The rules relating to real property are very complex, and many different people can have an interest in a particular piece of land. Thus there may be co-owners, equitable owners, and persons with rights arising from **leases, mortgages** or **easements**. The law orders the relationships between these different rights and lays down detailed rules for their recognition and enforcement.

Restitution regulates the reversal of **unjust enrichment**, where one party has received a benefit at the expense of another, which the law regards as being unjustified. The law of restitution deals with the various reasons why enrichment might be unjust (for example, if money was paid by mistake) and how the situation can be rectified.

The **law of succession** deals with what happens to a person's property after his death. Within certain limits the deceased can influence this by leaving a valid will (the requirements for which are laid down by law); in the case of an **intestate death** statutes govern the transfer of property to the beneficiaries. Rules provide for the maintenance of dependants and the correct administration of the estate.

Tax law, also called **revenue law**, covers all aspects of the United Kingdom tax system. It is therefore concerned with the interpretation of relevant legislation (for example as to the meaning of 'income' for the purposes of income tax), the correct administration of the various taxes, and the prohibition of **tax evasion**.

III. Terminology

Copyright: property right which allows a person (usually the author) to control the publication and sale of artistic works and ideas, such as literature, music and sound recordings.

Duty of confidentiality: subject to some exceptions, information such as personal information on the customer or details about his account, must not be passed on by the bank to third parties.

Duty of disclosure: the insured must provide the insurer will all material information. In general contract law, there is no such duty to volunteer information.

Easement: a right belonging to the owner of one piece of land, which relates to a different, neighbouring property. A common example is a right of way, which entitles the owner of property A to walk across property B.

Environment: air, water and land.

Insurance: a contract under which one party (the **insurer**) agrees to pay another (the **insured**) a certain amount of money, should a particular event occur. It must be unknown to both parties if, or in some cases when, the event will occur.

Intestate death: death of a person who has not made a will, or whose will is not valid.

Judicial review: the court cannot review the substantive decision (e.g. as to whether a particular individual is entitled to receive a certain benefit), but only the way in which the decision was reached.

Land: includes buildings and **fixtures**, that is things which have been attached to the land in such a way that they are regarded as being part of it (e.g. a fence).

Lease: contract by which the **tenant** (or **lessee**) is given the right to exclusive possession of land belonging to the **landlord** (or **lessor**) for a certain period of time. The tenant will usually pay **rent**.

Maternity rights: collection of rights a female employee has against her employer when she is pregnant or has just given birth, such as the right to time off work and to statutory maternity pay.

Minor: person under the age of 18.

Mortgage: legal arrangement by which land (or other property) is used as a security for a loan. The owner of the property is the **mortgagor**, the person who provides the loan is the **mortgagee**. If the load is not repaid as agreed, ownership in the land will pass to the mortgagee.

Murder: it is interesting to note there is no statutory definition of murder.

Patent: right given to a person to control the making, use and sale of an invention.

Premium: the amount of money the insured has to pay to the insurer every year to keep the insurance contract running.

Tax evasion: illegal non-payment of tax. This must be distinguished from **tax avoidance**, which refers to looking for legitimate ways of reducing the amount of tax payable.

Trade mark: a legally registered symbol, such as a name or design, that clearly identifies a connection between goods and a person or company.

Unjust enrichment: this does not mean that it is somehow 'unfair' that one party received a benefit; it means that there is no adequate legal basis for the transaction in question.

Index

acceptance 90, 114
acknowledgement of service 62
Act of God 106, 112
Act of Parliament 28
Act of Settlement 1700 52
acte clair doctrine 138
action 17
actionable *per se* 102
actual undue influence 94
Additional Member System 73
adequate consideration 89
administrative law 139
Admiralty Court 39
admission 62
ADR 45
adversarial system 46
advocacy 55
advocate 52
Advocate General 131
affirmation 92
agency 92, 110
agent 92, 110
aggravated damages 106
aggravated trespass 102
AGM 123
agreement to sell 109
alien 71
allocation questionnaire 60
allotment 122
allotted capital 123
allow an appeal 40
alternative dispute resolution 45
amendment 73
annual general meeting 123
anticipatory breach 95
appeal 37
appeal against sentence 40
appeal on point of fact 40
appeal on point of law 40
appellant 42
Appellate Committee of the House of Lords 40
appellate jurisdiction 37
applicant 64
application notice 64
appointment, judges 52
appointment, life peers 71
apportionment of damages 100
apprentices-at-law 25
arbitration 45
argot 17
Article 234 reference 134
articles of association 120
artificial person 119
ascertained goods 111
assault 102
Assembly, London 77
Assembly, Wales 74
assets 124
assignment 98
Assize of Novel Disseisin 20
attorney 25
Attorney-General 55
Attorney-General's Reference 38
attornment 112
authorised capital 122
authorised checks 48
automatic resulting trust 84
avoidance 92
award (arbitration) 45

backbenchers 77
bailment 110
balance of probabilities 50
banking law 139
Bar 54
Bar Council 55
Bar Final Examination 54
Bar Standards Board 55
Bar Vocational Course 54
bare legal title 86
bargain 89
barrister 54
barter 110
battery 102
bench 52
beneficial title 86
beneficiary 83
benefit 89
best endeavours 112
beyond reasonable doubt 50
bilateral contract 89
bill 72
Bill of Rights 1689 67
binding case 30
Blackacre 17
Blackstone, William 28
board of management 120
bona fide 121
books of authority 28
borough council 77
breach 95

breach of the peace 19
brief counsel 55
British Commonwealth 74
British Empire 23
budget (EC) 128
burden of proof 49
but-for test 99
buyer 109
BVC 54
by-election 71
by-law 29

cabinet 72
cab-rank rule 55
call to the Bar 54
candidate 71
canon law 28
capacity 93
capital 122
carelessness 103
carriage of goods 116
case law 30
case management 60
case management conference 61
case reporting 31
causation 99
Central Criminal Court 38
CEO 121
certainty of intention 87
certainty of objects 87
certainty of subject-matter 87
certificate of incorporation 120
cestui que trust 85
CFI 131
CFSP 127
Chamber of ECJ 131
Chambers 55
Chancellor 78
Chancellor of the Exchequer 72
Chancellor of the High Court 39
Chancery 78
Chancery Division 39
Channel Islands 23
charge having equivalent effect 134
charitable trust 84
Charities Act 2006 84
Charter of Fundamental Rights of the European Union 133
chattel 110
cheque 113
chief executive officer 121
Chief Whip 72
chose in action 111
chose in possession 111
CIF 118
circuit 21, 38
circuit judge 38
citation of cases 36
city council 77
civil case 37
Civil Division 40
civil jurisdiction 37
civil law 139
civil law system 19
Civil Procedure Rules 1998 60
civil procedure, pre-trial 60
Civil Service Tribunal 131
Civil War 22
claim form 61
claimant 61
class meeting 123
classification of companies 119
classification of contract terms 91
classification of law 139
classification of offences 44
clean hands principle 79
clerk of the court 37
code 30
code of practice 33
co-decision procedure 130
codified law 30
codifying statute 33
Coke, Sir Edward 28
collateral contract 109
Commercial Court 39
commercial law 109
Commission 128
commissioner 1268
Committee of Permanent Representatives of the Member States 128
Committee of the Regions 129
Common Foreign and Security Policy 127
common law 19
common law courts 20
common mistake 93
common position 130
Common Professional Examination 53
Commonwealth 71
Commonwealth of Nations 74
Companies Act 2006 119
company 119
company limited by guarantee 119
company limited by shares 119
complete defence 105
complete jurisdiction 79
complete legal title 117

composition of the jury 47
compulsory winding-up 124
conciliation 45
Conciliation Committee 130
concurrent liability 99
condition 91
conditional contract 96
conditional fee agreement 65
conditional payment 113
conflict of interests 121
conflict of laws 139
consent 105
consideration 89
constituency 71
constitution 7656
Constitution for Europe 127
constitution of a company 120
constitutional convention 67
constitutional court 29, 37
constitutional law 67
Constitutional Reform Act 2005 37, 52
constitutive Treaties 131
construction law 139
construction of a statute 33
constructive trust 84
consultation procedure 129
consumer contracts 109
contempt of court 62
contingency fee 65
contract 88
contract for sale 109
contract for services 110
contributories 124
contributory negligence 100
convergence criteria 135
co-operation procedure 130
copyright 140
COREPER 128
corporation tax 126
correspondent bank 114
cost, insurance and freight 118
costs 60
council 76
Council (of Ministers) 128
Council of Europe 136
Council of the European Union 128
council tax 77
councillor 76
counsel 55
counterclaim 62
counter-offer 98
county 19
county council 77
county court 22, 38
Court of Appeal 40
Court of Assize 21
Court of Auditors 129
Court of Chancery 78
Court of Common Pleas 21
Court of Exchequer 20
Court of First Instance 131
Court of King's Bench 21
Court of Star Chamber 21
court structure, diagram of 42
court system 37
CPE 53
CPR 60
CPS 56
CRA 2005 37, 52
credit 109
credit card 113
creditor 122
criminal case 37
Criminal Division 40
criminal jurisdiction 37
Criminal Justice Act 2003 47
criminal law 140
Cromwell, Oliver 22
cross-appeal 42
cross-bencher 72
Crown 68
Crown Court 38
Crown Prosecution Service 56
culpability 100
curia advisari vult 17
Curia Regis 20
custom 27
customs duties 134

damages 95, 104
de minimis non lex curat 113
debenture 126
decision (EC law) 132
declaration of incompatibility 29
deductive reasoning 30
deed 90
defamation 100
default judgment 63
defaulting trustee 85
defence 62, 105
defendant 61
deferral 47
deferred shares 122
delegated legislation 29
delivery 111

Department for Children, Schools and Families 72
Department of Health 72
Deputy First Minister 74
derivative action 123
description of goods 113
despatch box 77
detriment 89
devolution 73
devolved matters 73
Dicey, Albert Venn 668
direct applicability 133
direct effect 133
direction to jury 50
directions 60
directions timetable 61
directive 132
director 120
Director of Public Prosecutions 56
disclosure 63
discretionary excusal 47
discretionary reference 134
discretionary remedy 80
discrimination 128
dismiss an appeal 40
disproportionate measure 133
disqualification 47
dissenting opinion 41
dissolution of a company 124
dissolution of Parliament 68
distinguish 32
district 38
district council 77
district judge 37
dividend 121
Division 39, 40
Divisional Court 39
doctrine of precedent 31
doctrine *of stare decisis* 30
document 63
document of title 122
documentary credit 114
Donoghue v Stevenson 108
double jeopardy 49
DPP 56
duress 94
duty of care 103
duty of disclosure 94, 140

easement 140
ECB 135
ECJ 130
Economic and Monetary Union 135
Economic and Social Committee 129
economic duress 94
economic loss 103
ECOSOC 129
ECSC 127
EEC 127
EGM 123
eiusdem generis rule 30
election (contract law) 92
electoral register 71
electoral system 71
electorate 71
Employment Appeal Tribunal 40
employment law 140
employment tribunal 43
EMU 135
enabling statute 29
England 23
entrenchment 69
environmental law 140
equitable estoppel 86
equitable maxim 79
equitable owner 82
equitable remedy 80
equitable title 83
equity 78
estate 39
estoppel 86
EU 127
Euratom 127
euro 135
European Assembly 136
European Atomic Energy Community 127
European Central Bank 135
European Coal and Steel Community 127
European Communities Act 1972 127
European Community law 127
European Convention for the Protection of Human Rights and Fundamental Freedoms 133
European Council 128
European Court of Human Rights 136
European Court of Justice 130
European Economic Community 127
European institutions 128
European Parliament 129
European Union 127
euro-zone 135
evidence 63
ex turpi causa non oritur actio 105
ex works 118
exchange of documents 63
Exchequer 20, 21

exclusion clause 91
excusal 47
executed consideration 90
executed document 17
executed sale 117
executed use 82
executive 70
Executive Committee 74
executive function 70
executory consideration 90
executory contract of sale 117
exemplary damages 105
exemption clause 91
existing goods 111
expert witness 63
express term 90
extraordinary general meeting 123

false imprisonment 102
Family Division 39
family law 140
FAS 118
fast track 61
fault 102
fealty 21
fiduciary 85
fiduciary relationship 85
file an admission 62
final injunction 81
financial eligibility 64
financial loss 104
fines 37
firm of solicitors 53
first class post 62
first instance 37
First Lord of the Treasury 75
First Minister 73, 74
first past the post 71
first reading 73
fixture 141
FOB 118
force majeure 112
foreman of the jury 49
form 90
Foss v Harbottle 123
founders' shares 122
Francovich principle 138
fraud on the minority 123
fraudulent misrepresentation 94
free alongside ship 118
free movement of capital 135
free movement of goods 134
free movement of services 135
free movement of workers 135
free on board 118
freedom of contract 88
freedom of establishment 135
freedom of speech 105
freezing injunction 81
frontbencher 77
frustration 95
full court 40
Full Court of ECJ 131
full legal owner 82
fusion of law and equity 79
future goods 111

General Court 131
general defence 105
general election 71
general meeting 123
general principles of law 132
gift 89, 109
Glorious Revolution 22
going concern 119
golden rule 30
Good Friday Agreement 74
good title 111
goods 110
government 72
Government bill 73
government department 72
governor 120
Grand Chamber 131
grand jury 46
gratuitous gift 89, 109
Gray‘s Inn 54
Great Britain 23, 67
Greater London Authority 77
green paper 76
grounds for appeal 40

help at court 64
Her Majesty's Opposition 8736
hereditary peer 71
High Court 39
High Court judge 39
highway 101
hire-purchase agreement 110
hold on trust 83
Home Office 72
honouring of cheque 113
horizontal direct effect 134
host state 135
House of Commons 70
House of Lords 40, 71

House of Lords Act 1999 71
Houses of Parliament 70
Human Rights Act 1998 29
human rights law 139
hundreds 19
hybrid legal system 23

illegality 93, 105
immunity 53, 68
implementation 132
implied term 90
imprisonment 37
in argument 28
in breach 95
in default 63, 85
in equity 83
in law 83
in lieu 18
in private 48
incorporated company 119
Incorporated Council of Law Reporting for England and Wales 31
independent judges 53
Independent Selection Panel 55
indictable offence 45
indirect effect 138
inductive reasoning 30
industrial law 140
ineligibility 47
initiating proceedings 61
injunction 81
Inner Temple 54
innocent misrepresentation 94
innominate term 91
Inns of Court 25, 54
inquisitorial system 46
insolvency 119
insolvent liquidation 124
inspection 63
instalments 113
instrument 17
insurance 140
intellectual property law 140
intention 103
intention to create legal relations 90
interim injunction 81
intermediate term 91
internal market 134
international law 139
interpret a statute 29, 30
Interpretation Act 1978 30
interpretation section 30
Interregnum 22
intestate death 141
intra vires 29
investigation 56
invitation to treat 98
Isle of Man 23
issued capital 123
issuing bank 114
itinerant judge 21

JCSB 47
joint text 130
jointly liable 126
judge 52
judgment in default 63
judgment without trial 63
Judicature Acts 1873-75 22, 37
Judicial Appointments Commission 52
judicial authority 38
Judicial Committee of the Privy Council 31, 41
judicial immunity 53
judicial independence 53
judicial interpretation 30
judicial panels 131
judicial review 29, 139
judiciary 70
junior minister 72
juristic person 119
juror 47
jury 46
jury box 49
Jury Central Summoning Bureau 47
jury room 49
jury secrecy 49
jury service 47
jury system 46
jury tampering 49
jury trial 49
jury vetting 47
jus gentium 139
Justices of the Supreme Court 41
justification by law 106

King's Bench Division 43

labour law 140
laches 79
land law 140
landlord 141
language 17
Law Commission 118
law degree 53
law journal 33

Law Lords 40
law merchant 28
law of nations 139
law officers 55
law report 31
law review 33
Law Society 54
lawyer 53
lay magistrate 37
lay person 43
lay witness 63
LC 70
LCJ 40
Leader of the Opposition 75
leapfrog procedure 39
lease 140
leave to appeal 43
legal aid 64
legal causation 100
legal certainty 132
legal duty to take care 103
legal help 64
legal owner 82
legal personnel 52
Legal Practice Course 53
legal profession 26, 53
legal remedy 80
legal representation 64
legal security 137
Legal Services Commission 64
legal sources of law 67
legal title 83
legal treatise 28
legally enforceable obligation 88
legislation 28
legislative framework 29
legislative function 70
legislative process 72
legislative process (EU) 129
legislature 70
legitimate expectation 132
lessee 141
lessor 141
letter of credit 114
liability 99
libel 100
licence 106
Licensed Access 55
lien 115
life peer 71
limited company 124
Limited Liability Partnership 54, 126
Lincoln's Inn 54
liquidation 124
liquidator 124
listing questionnaire 61
literal rule 30
LJ 58
LLPs 54
local authority 76
local election 76
local government 76
local jurisdiction 38
locality 27
lodge an appeal 37
Lord Chancellor 70
Lord Chief Justice 40
Lord Justice of Appeal 40
Lord President of the Council 41
Lord Protector 24
Lord Speaker 70
Lords of Appeal in Ordinary 40
Lords Spiritual 71
Lords Temporal 71
loss of amenities 105
loss of earnings 105
loss of enjoyment of life 106
Lower House 70
loyalists 75
LPC 53

Maastricht Agreement 127
magistrates' court 37
Magna Carta 21, 67
majority rule 123
majority verdict 49
malperformance 95
management track 60
managing director 121
mandamus 21
mandatory injunction 80
manifesto 72
Master of the Rolls 40
maternity rights 140
Mayor of London 77
means test 64
measure having equivalent effect 134
media law 139
mediation 45
medical expenses 105
Member of Parliament 70
Member of Scottish Parliament 73
Member of the European Parliament 129
Member of Welsh Assembly 74
Member State 127
Members of the Legislative Assembly 74

membership of a company 121
memorandum of association 120
MEP 129
merchantable quality 118
metropolitan area 77
metropolitan district council 77
Middle Temple 54
migrant worker 135
minister (Scotland) 73
minister (Wales) 74
minister of state 72
minister of the Crown 72
minor 93, 140
minutes 121
mirror image rule 98
mischief rule 30
misconduct 54
misrepresentation 94
mistake 93
monetary compensation 95
money bill 73
moot court 26
mortgage 140
movables 110
MP 70
MR 40
MSP 73
multi-track 61
murder 140
mutual mistake 93

nationalists 74
necessity 105
negligence 103
negligent misrepresentation 94
negotiable instrument 111
neighbour principle 108
nervous shock 103
neutral citation 36
nolle prosequi 55
nominal consideration 89
nominal damages 102
non-disclosure 94
non-Member State 131
non-metropolitan area 77
non-pecuniary loss 104
non-performance 95
non-privileged party 131
Northern Ireland 23, 74
Northern Ireland Assembly 74
notice of allocation 60
nuisance 101

obiter dicta 31
obligatory reference 134
of the essence 112
offence triable either way 45
offer 88
Old Bailey 38
on notice 81
on risk 114
opinion (EC law) 132
opposition 72
option 110
ordeal by fire 20
ordeal by water 20
Order in Council 29
ordinary legislative procedure 130
ordinary shares 122
original jurisdiction 37
overrule 32
ownership 111

pain and suffering 105
Palace of Westminster 70
panel 40, 47, 131
parent act 29
parish council 77
Parliament 70
parliamentary sovereignty 69
parliamentary supremacy 69
Part 36 Payment 66
partial defence 105
particulars of claim 62
partnership 54, 119
party 17
passing of statute 72
patent 140
Patent Court 39
payment 113
payment into court 66
pecuniary loss 104
peerage 71
peppercorn consideration 89
performance 95
permission to appeal 40
perpetual injunction 81
personal action 115, 130
personal chattel 110
personal injury 103
personal property 117
personalty 117
persuasive authority 29
petition 78
petty crime 37
petty jury 46

PgDL 53
physical damage 103
physical transfer 112
pillory 21
place of business 38
place of residence 38
plaintiff 78
pleader 25
plenary session 136
PM 72
Police and Judicial Co-operation in Criminal Matters 127
possession 111
Postgraduate Diploma in Law 53
power to resell 115
power to transfer title 111
powers of the Crown 68
Practice Directions 60
pre-action protocol 65
precedent 30
preferential shares 122
preliminary ruling 134
prerogative of pardon 68
prerogative order 39
prerogative power 68
prerogative writ 21
President, Family Division 39
President, Queen's Bench Division 39
President, Supreme Court 41
presumed resulting trust 85
presumption 34
pre-trial civil procedure 60
pre-trial review 61
price 109
primary legislation 28
Prime Minister 72
principal 92, 110
private bill 72
private company 120
private express trust 83
private international law 139
private law 139
Private Member's bill 73
private nuisance 101
privilege 68, 106
privity of contract 92
Privy Council 41
Professional Skills Course 54
prohibition 21
prohibitory injunction 80
promisee 89
promisor 89
promissory estoppel 86
promoter 120
property 114
property damage 103
proportional representation 73
proportionality 133
proprietary estoppel 86
prosecution process 56
prospectus 126
proxy 126
psychiatric illness 103
Public Access 55
public bill 72
public company 119
public international law 139
public law 139
puisne judge 39
punitive damages 105
pupillage 55
pur autre vie 18
pure economic loss 104
purpose trust 84
purpose, fitness for 113

QC 55
qualified majority vote 128
qualified solicitor 53
quality 113
quantitative restriction 134
quash 40
Queen in Parliament 70
Queen's Bench Division 39
Queen's Counsel 55
quota 137

raise to the bench 56
ratio decidendi 31
real property 117
real remedy 115
realise assets 124
realty 117
reasonableness 28, 107
reasonable person 103
reasonably foreseeable 108
recipocity 89
recommendation 132
recorder 38
rectification 81
refer to ECJ 134
Regina 44
register of members 121
registered company 119
Registrar of Companies 119
registration of company 119

regulation 29, 132
rejection 116
relational undue influence 94
relative majority method 71
relator action 55, 101
remedy 80, 95, 104, 115, 123
remoteness 100
removal of judges 52
reply 62
report 73
reporter 31
representation 90
representative action 123
representee 97
representor 97
republicans 75
repudiation 112
reputation 100
request-for-judgment procedure 63
resale 115
rescind 81, 92
rescission 81
reservation of title clause 117
reserved matters 73
resolution 120
respondent 42, 664
restitutio in integrum 81
restitution 96, 140
Restoration 22
resulting trust 84
re-tender 116
retention of title clause 115
retroactivity 132
revenue law 141
Rex 44
right of audience 52
right of possession 114
right of stoppage in transit 115
right of way 27
right to resell 115
right to sell 111
rights of the Crown 68
risk 114
Royal Assent 72
royal courts 20
royal justice 20
royal prerogative 68
royalists 24
rule of law 67
rules of interpretation 30
rules of law 27
Rylands v Fletcher 102
sale 109
sale and supply of goods 109
sale by sample 113
Sale of Goods Act 1979 109
satisfactory quality 113
Scotland 23, 73
Scottish Government 73
Scottish Parliament 73
SEA 128
search order 81
seat in Parliament 71
second reading 73
secondary legislation 29
secondary victim 104
secretary of company 121
secretary of state 72
security of tenure 52
self-dealing 124
self-employed 135
seller 109
Senior Courts 37
separate dependencies 23
separation of powers 70
serjeants-at-law 25
service 135
service of documents 62
settlement out of court 60
settlor 83
SGA 1979 109
shadow cabinet 72
share 121
share capital 122
share certificate 122
shareholder 121
shire-moot 19
shires 19
Single European Act 128
single market 137
slander 101
small claims track 60
sole trader 119
solicitor 53
solicitor advocate 54
Solicitor-General 55
Solicitors Regulation Authority 54
solvent liquidation 124
sources of law 27
sovereign 69
Speaker 71
Speaker's Chair 77
special defence 105
special directions 61
specialised courts 131

specific disclosure 63
specific goods 111
specific performance 80, 96
spes 111
sponsored bill 73
stand by for the Crown 47
standard directions 61
standard disclosure 63
standard form 91
standard of proof 49
Standing Committee 73
stare decisis 30
statement of truth 62
statements of case 62
statute 28
Statute of Uses 1535 82
statutory company 119
statutory construction 33
statutory instrument 29
statutory interpretation 30
stock exchange 121
stocks 125
strict liability 102
subordinate legislation 29
subpoena 78
subscription 121
success fee 65
succession, law of 141
sufficient consideration 89
summary judgment 63
summary offence 45
summary trial 45
summing-up 49
summoning of jurors 47
summoning of Parliament 68
supervisory jurisdiction 39
Supreme Court 40
symbolic delivery 112

Table of the House 77
take delivery 114
take silk 55
tax law 141
tenancy 54
tenant 141
tenure 52
term of art 17
term, implied 90
term, keeping of 54
terminate contract 91
TEU 127
TFEU 127
thing in action 110
thing in possession 111
third reading 73
three certainties 87
three-line whip 76
time immemorial 27
time, stipulations as to 112
title 111
ToA 127
ToN 127
tort 99
tortfeasor 99
tortious liability 99
town council 77
tracing 85
trade union 140
trade union law 140
trade usage 27
trade mark 140
training contract 53
transcript 31
transfer of property 114
Treasury 20, 72
Treaty of Amsterdam 127
Treaty of Nice 127
Treaty of Rome 127
Treaty of the European Union 127
Treaty on the Functioning of the European Union 127
trespass 102
trial by battle 20
trial by jury 46
trial by ordeal 20
trial on indictment 45
trial system 46
trial window 61
tribunal 39
trust 82
trust fund 83
trustee 83

ultra vires 29
unanimous verdict 49
unascertained goods 111
unconditional contract 96
undue influence 94
unenforceable contract 92
unilateral contract 89
unilateral mistake 93
unionists 74
unitary authority 77
United Kingdom of Great Britain and Northern Ireland 23
universal adult franchise 71

unjust enrichment 140
unlimited company 125
unpaid seller 115
unpaid seller's lien 115
unwritten constitution 67
Upper House 71
use 82

valid consideration 89
validity 29, 69
verdict 49
vertical direct effect 134
vis major 106, 112
vocational training 53, 57
void 92
voidable 92
volenti non fit injuria 105
voluntary winding-up 124
vote of censure 129

Wales 23, 73
warranty 91
Welsh Assembly 74
Welsh Government 74
Westminster Parliament 73
Whip 72
white paper 76
Whiteacre 17
winding-up 124
without notice injunction 81
witness statement 61
Woolsack 77
World Trade Organisation 131
writ 78
writ of certiorari 21
written constitution 67
WTO 131, 152

Lingua Juris
Kompendien zu Recht und Terminologie

herausgegeben von Ute Goergen, FFA, Universität Trier